FOUR PIECES

π

UPON REFLECTION...

HYPERCANON
ANTICANON

●

by

GERALD BRENNAN

Dream Street Press

Ann Arbor, MI USA
www.DreamStreetPress.com

DREAM STREET PRESS
217 Sunset Rd.
Ann Arbor, MI 48103
www.DreamStreetPress.com

π

Upon Reflection...

Hypercanon

Anticanon

π

for chamber septet

by
Gerald Brennan
© 2022

π

I here endeavor to create a piece for septet that, more graciously and effectively than anything previously written, captures the sonic and the musical essence of π, the ratio of a circle's circumference to its diameter.

π is expressed as a non-repeating decimal of infinite length commonly approximated as 3.14159. This is a base$_{10}$ number, which would be swell to use if I decided to use 10 notes of our western musical scale. Since such a work as this is essentially the expression of a seemingly "random" number, there is therefore enough of what the average listener will perceive as "dissonance" already built into the work. I decided therefore to eliminate "sharps and flats" and stick to just the "white keys" on the piano, making the work purely diatonic, avoiding the use of chromaticism that would result in a much more grating listening experience.

Since I am using only 7 notes of the major/minor scale, I decided to convert π to a base₇ number. As I result, I was able to pair each number with a note of the scale. So, I now had a string of numbers that would supply the notes I needed to construct a melody. But how long of a string should I use? The number is, after all, infinitely long. The three most significant digits of π in base₇ are the first three: 306. So I would use the first 306 digits of π (in base₇ which is 313 in base₁₀) as the pitches of my melody.

I decided to use this resulting string of pitches, but what would be the note values? That is, how long should each note be played?

To solve this, I retrograded the string of numbers that I used to derive pitch (that means I ran it backwards) and paired each pitch number with the new duration number in the retrograde table. I simply assigned each duration number with that number of beats. For example, pairing the first number in the pitch string (3, which is always assigned Bb), with the last number of the pitch string (the first number when inverted into the new duration string; 5, indicating 5 beats) means a Bb which is held for 5 beats.

Repeating this function 313 times till all numbers from the two tables are paired, gives me my melody.

So what do I do with this melody? I assigned it to 7 diverse instruments in order to minimize homogeneity. Each plays the same melody, simply beginning at different times. In musicspeak, this is called a "canon."

I used the first few digits of π in base$_7$ to assign in what order the instruments enter, and at what point in the piece does each instrument enter in.

π_7 is used in its simplest ways to derive every technical and musical aspect of this work.

For the very curious, the complete technical specs are available upon request.

Finally, I hope you enjoy the music. As music.

Gerald Brennan
April 12, 2015
Ann Arbor, MI USA

π

Score

π

for septet

Gerald Brennan

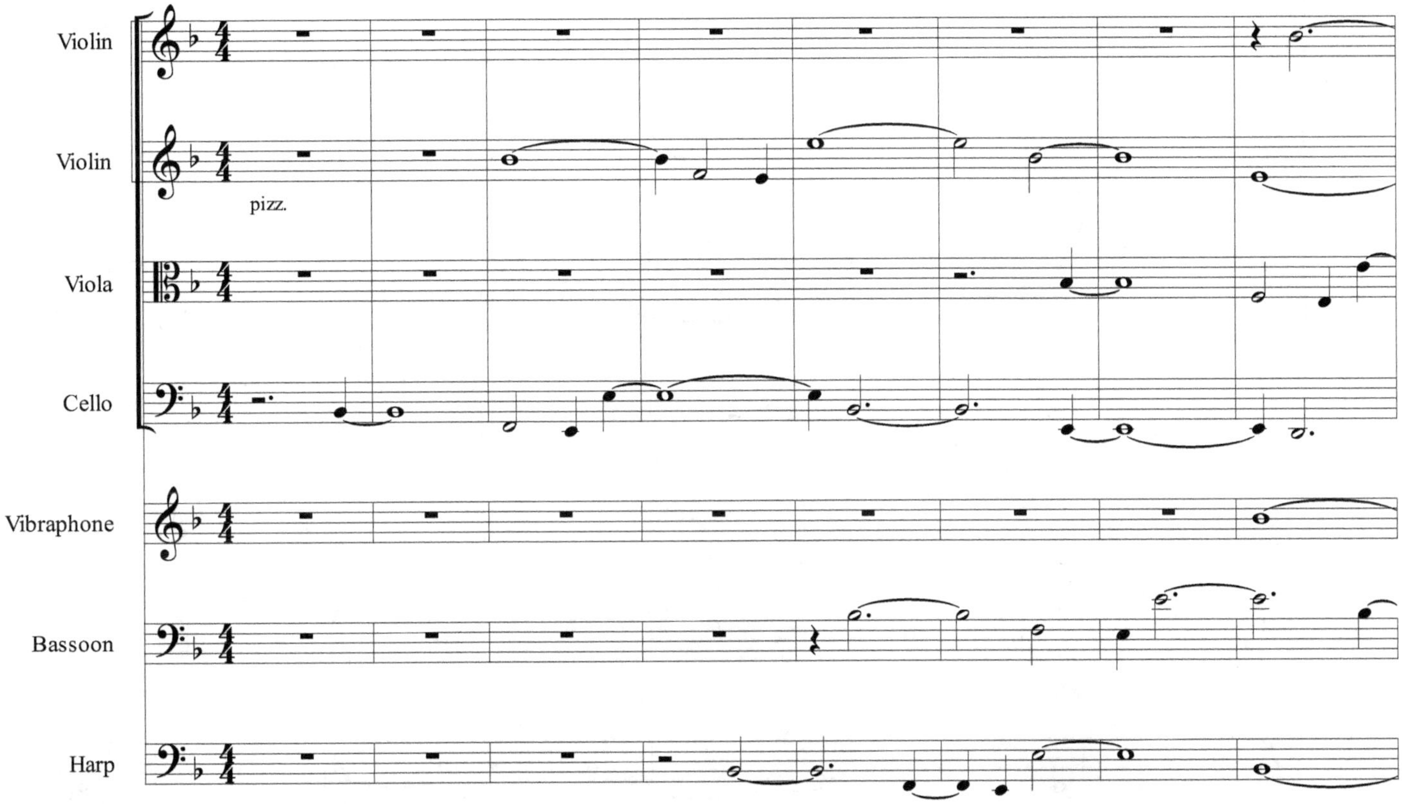

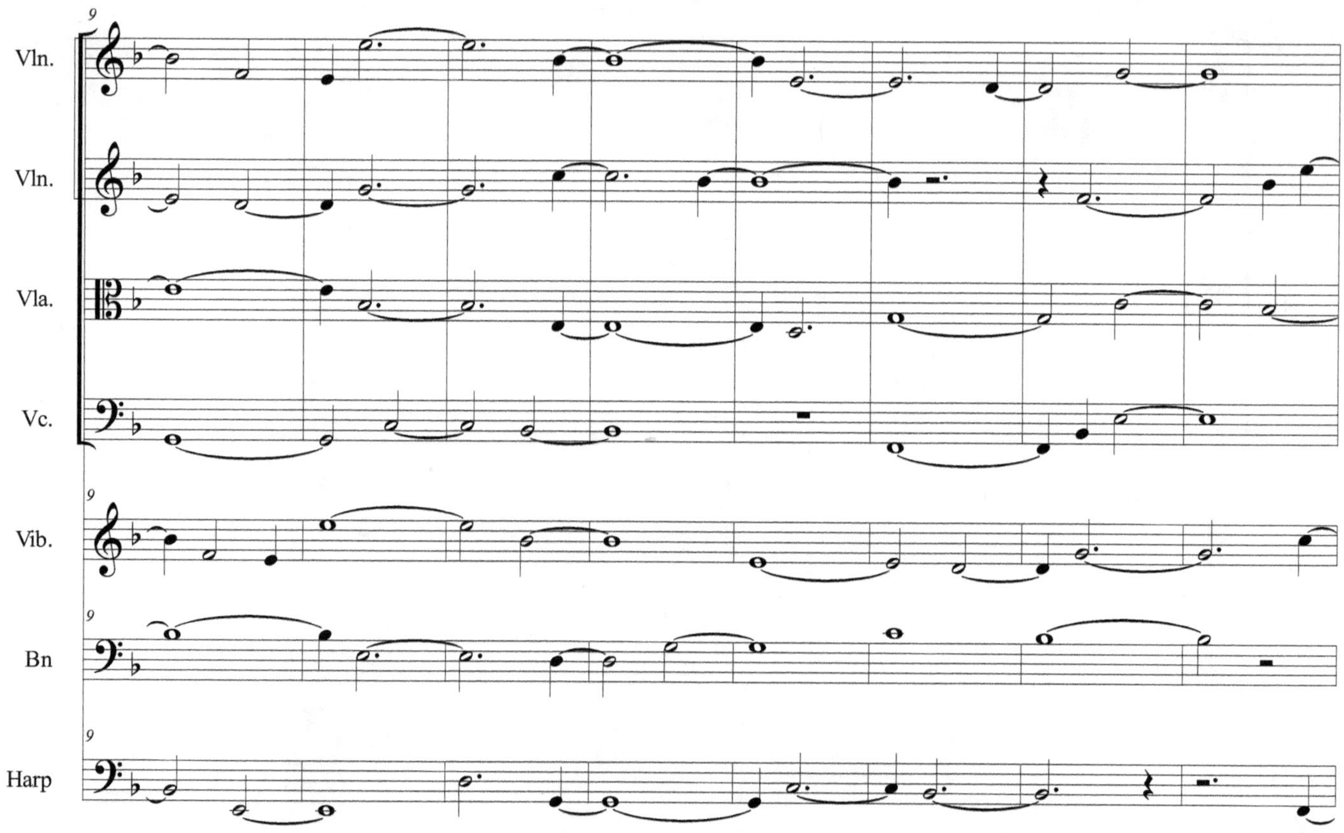
9
Vln.
Vln.
Vla.
Vc.
Vib.
Bn
Harp

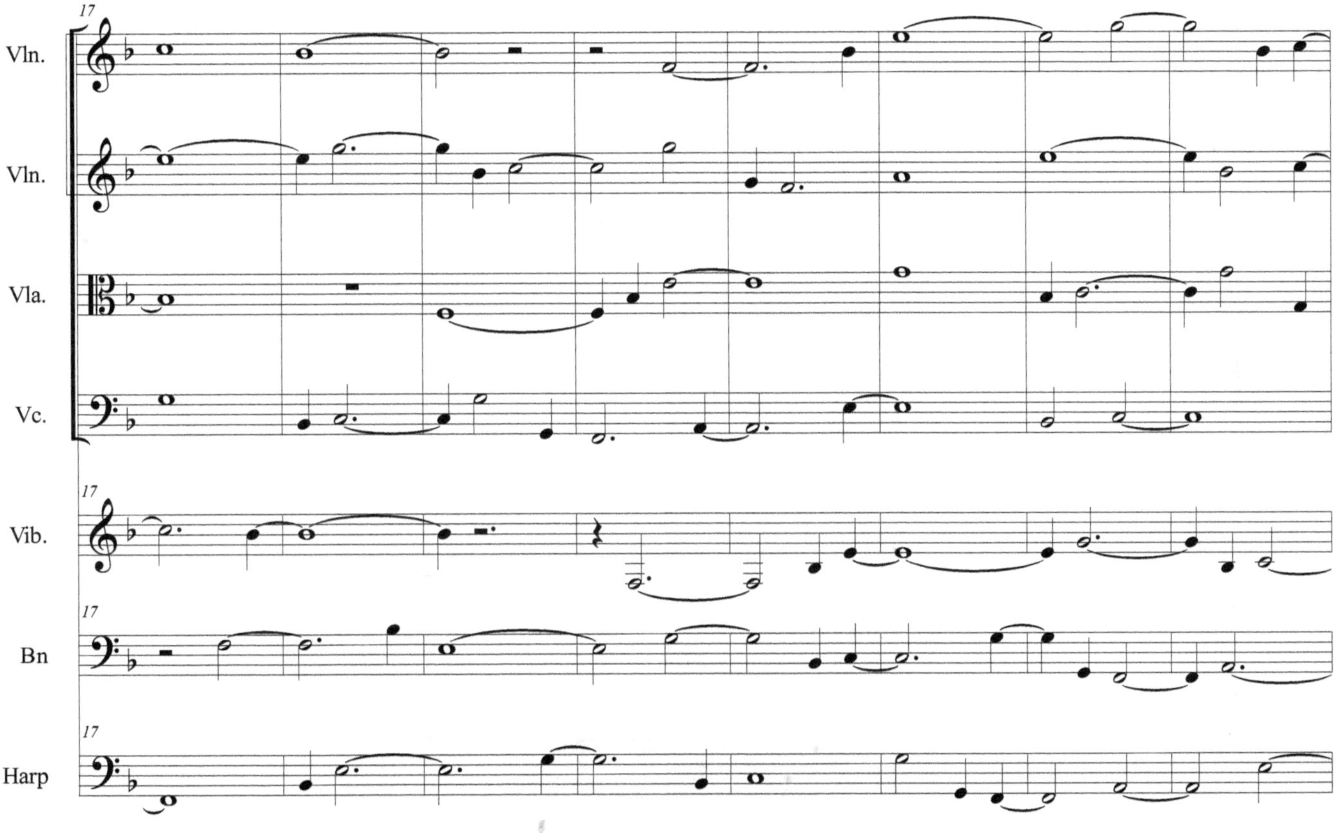
17
Vln.
Vln.
Vla.
Vc.
17
Vib.
17
Bn
17
Harp

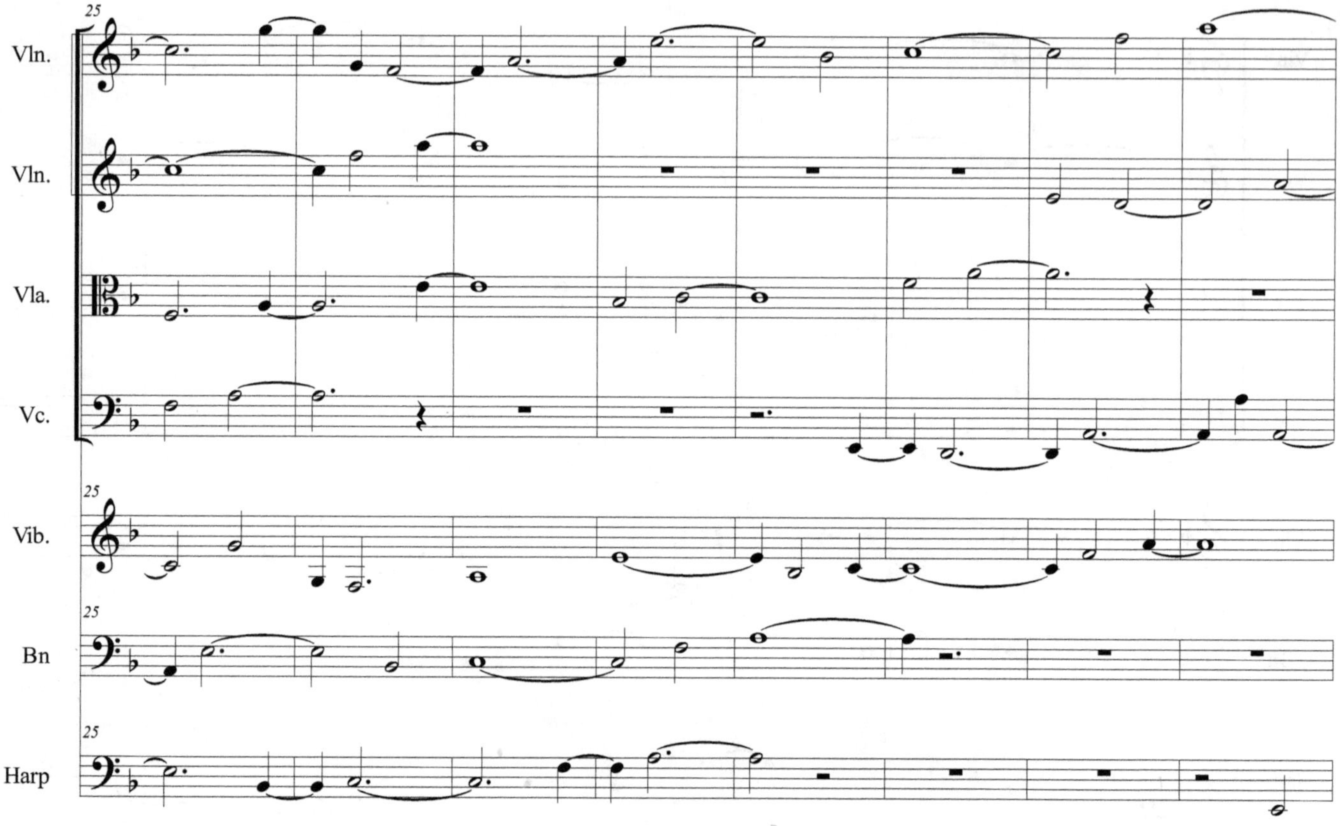
25
Vln.
Vln.
Vla.
Vc.
25
Vib.
25
Bn
25
Harp

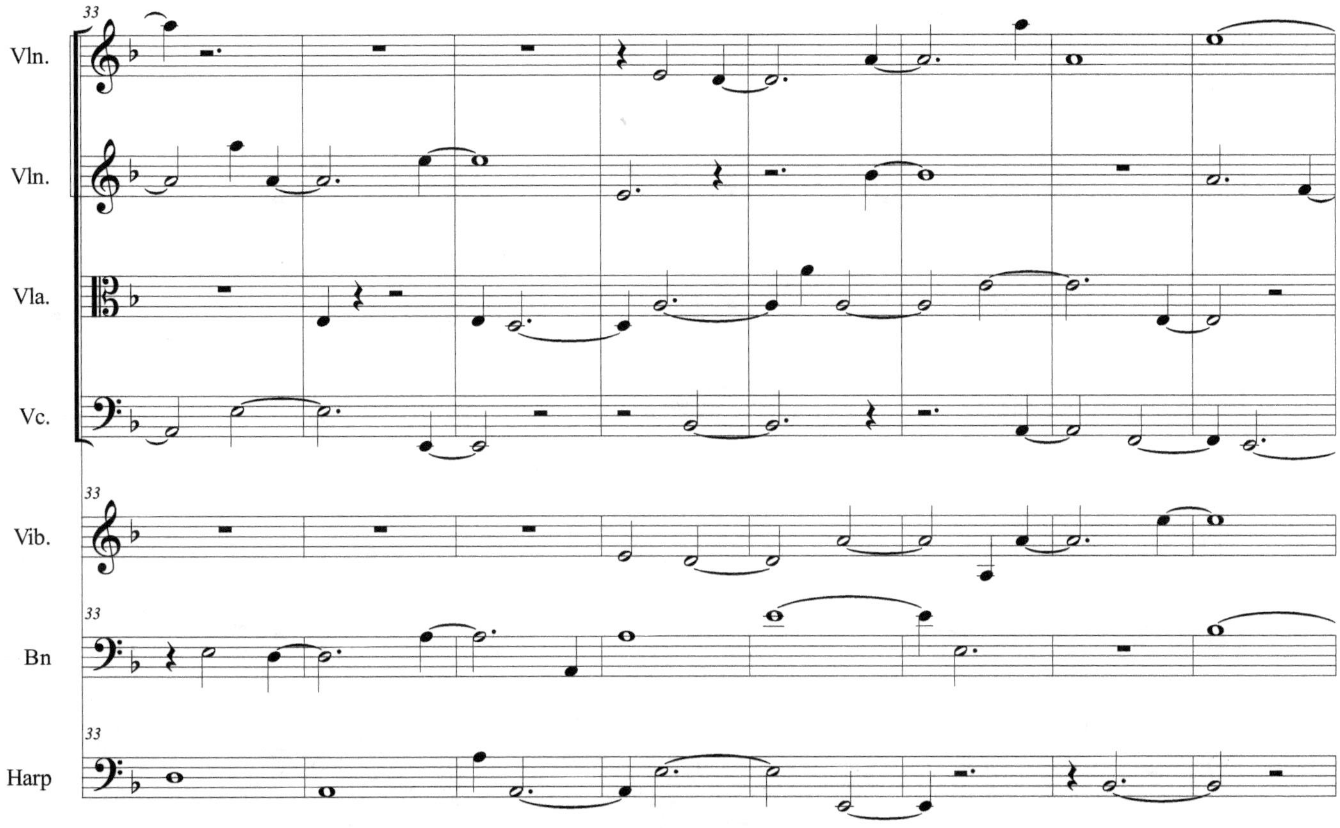
33
Vln.
Vln.
Vla.
Vc.
33
Vib.
33
Bn
33
Harp

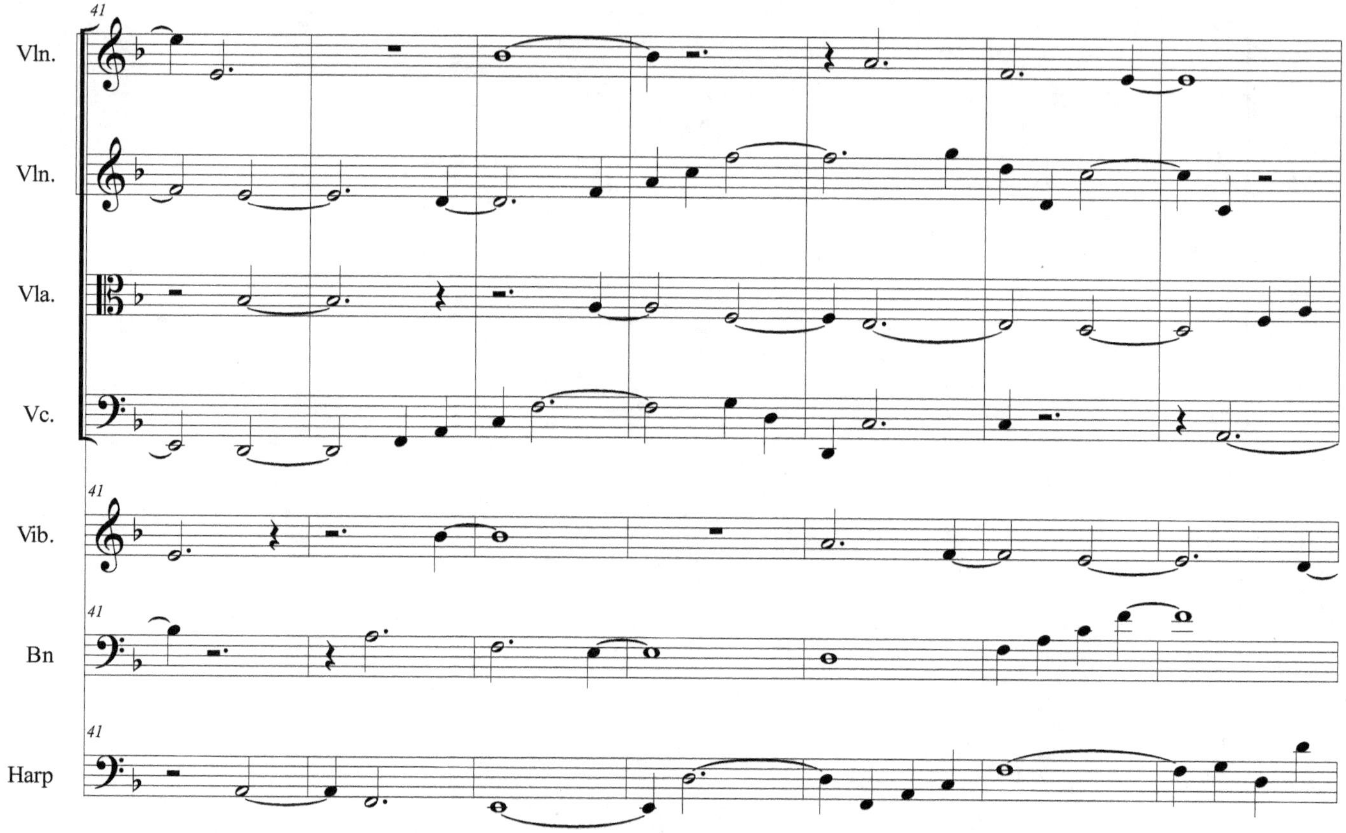
41
Vln.
Vln.
Vla.
Vc.
41
Vib.
41
Bn
41
Harp

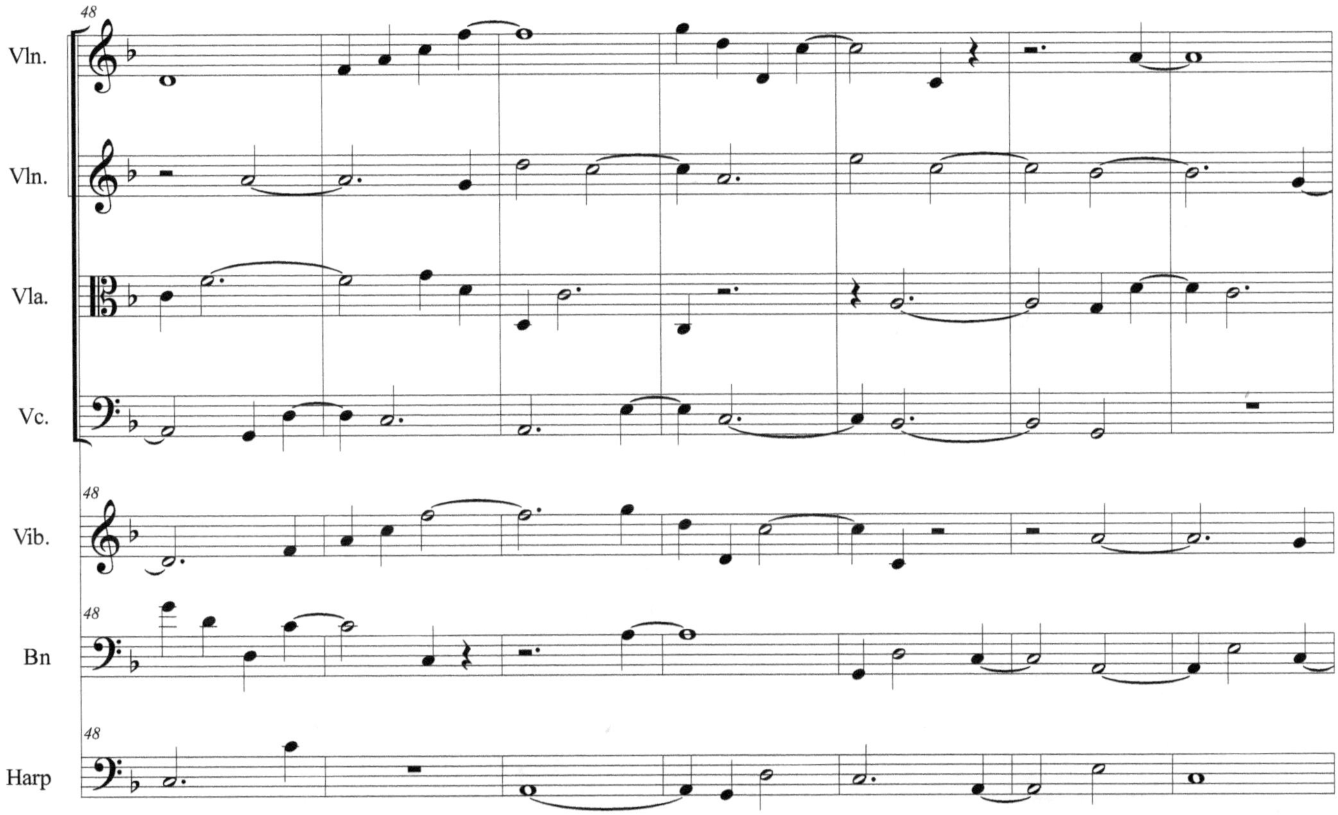
48
Vln.
Vln.
Vla.
Vc.
48
Vib.
48
Bn
48
Harp

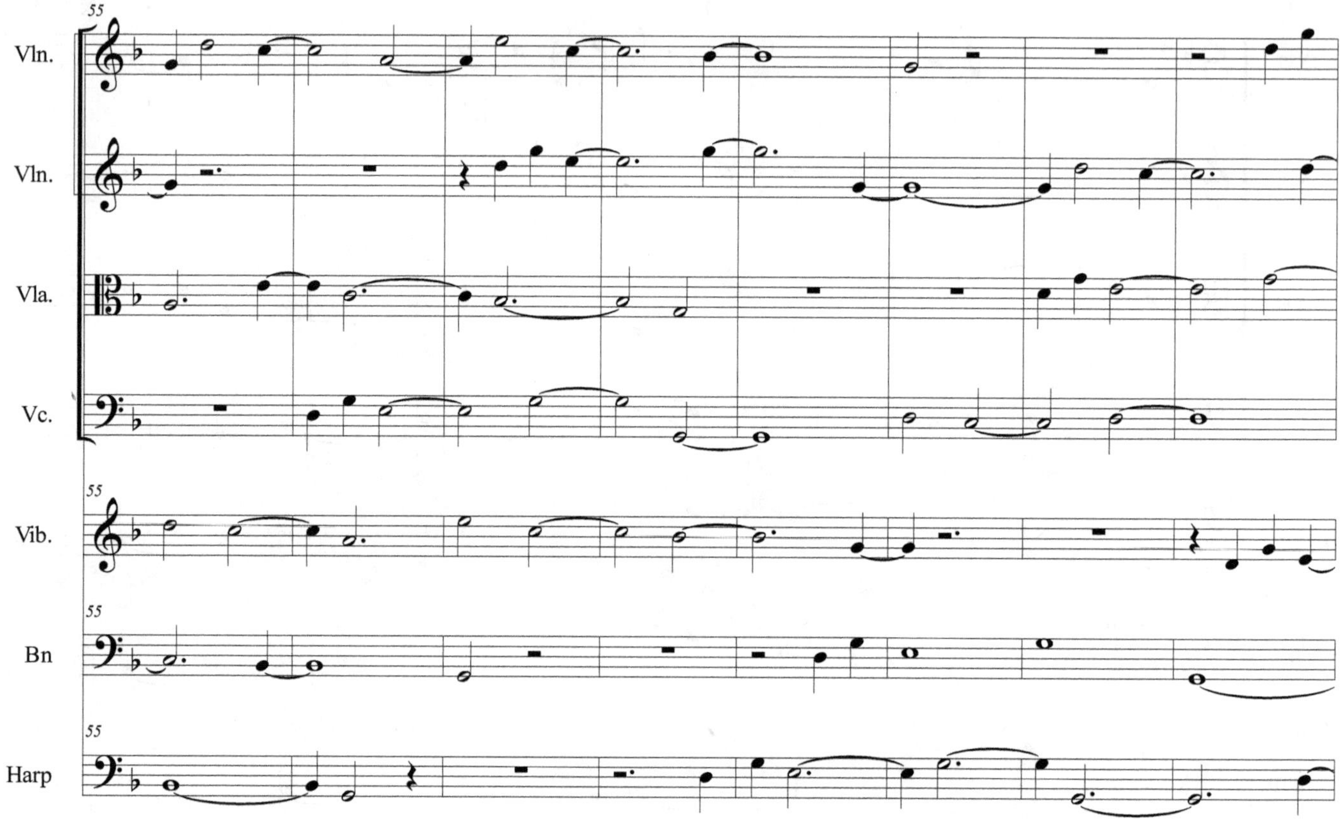
55
Vln.
Vln.
Vla.
Vc.
55
Vib.
55
Bn
55
Harp

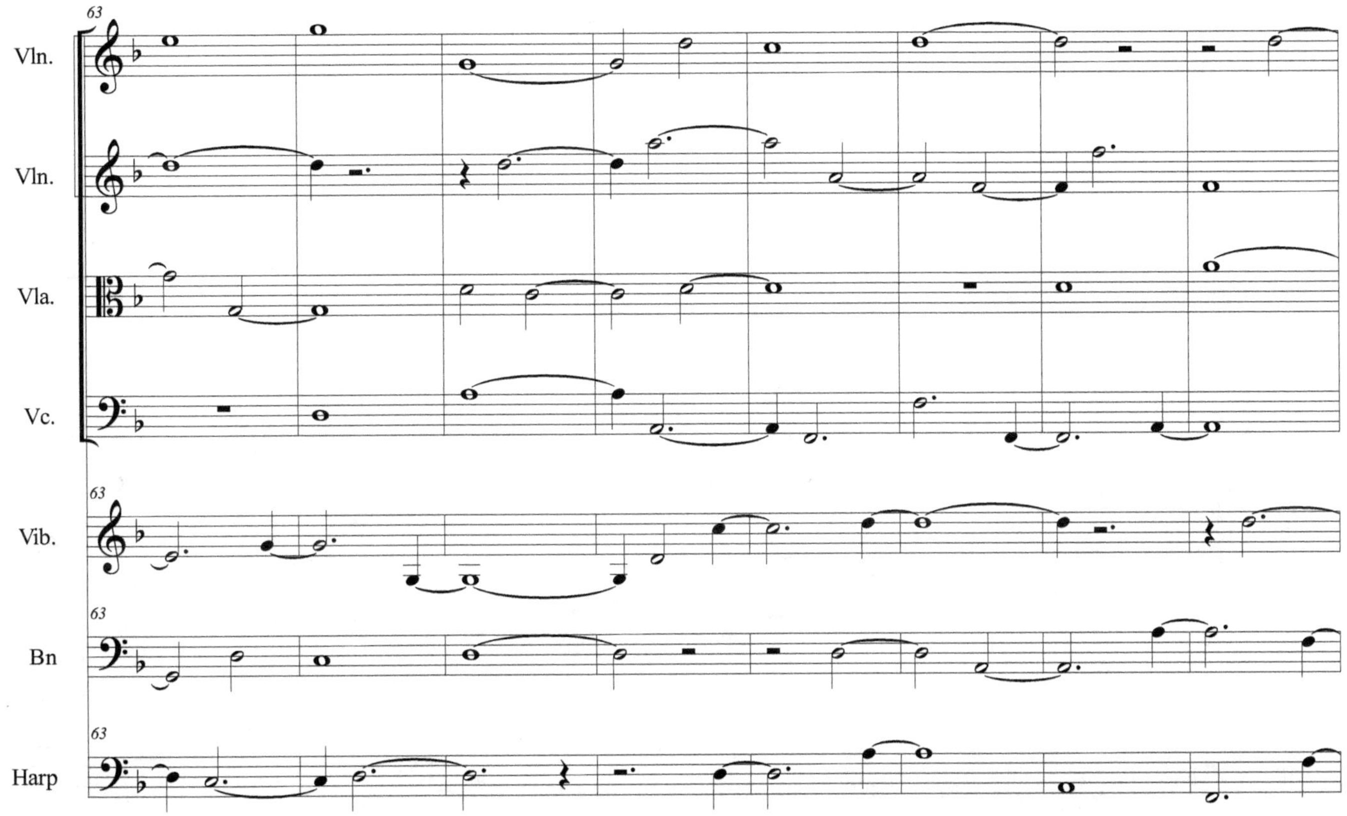
63
Vln.
Vln.
Vla.
Vc.
63
Vib.
63
Bn
63
Harp

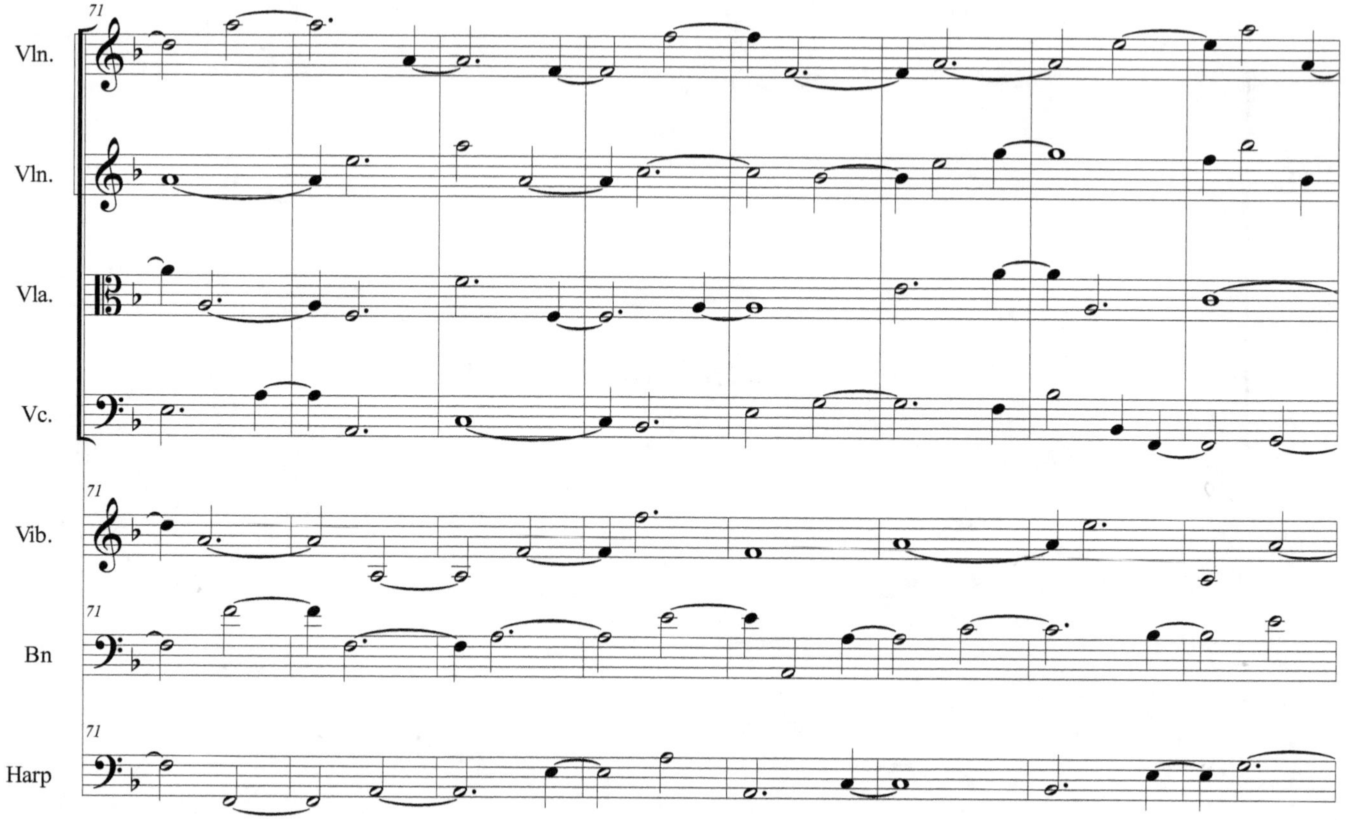
71
Vln.
Vln.
Vla.
Vc.
71
Vib.
71
Bn
71
Harp

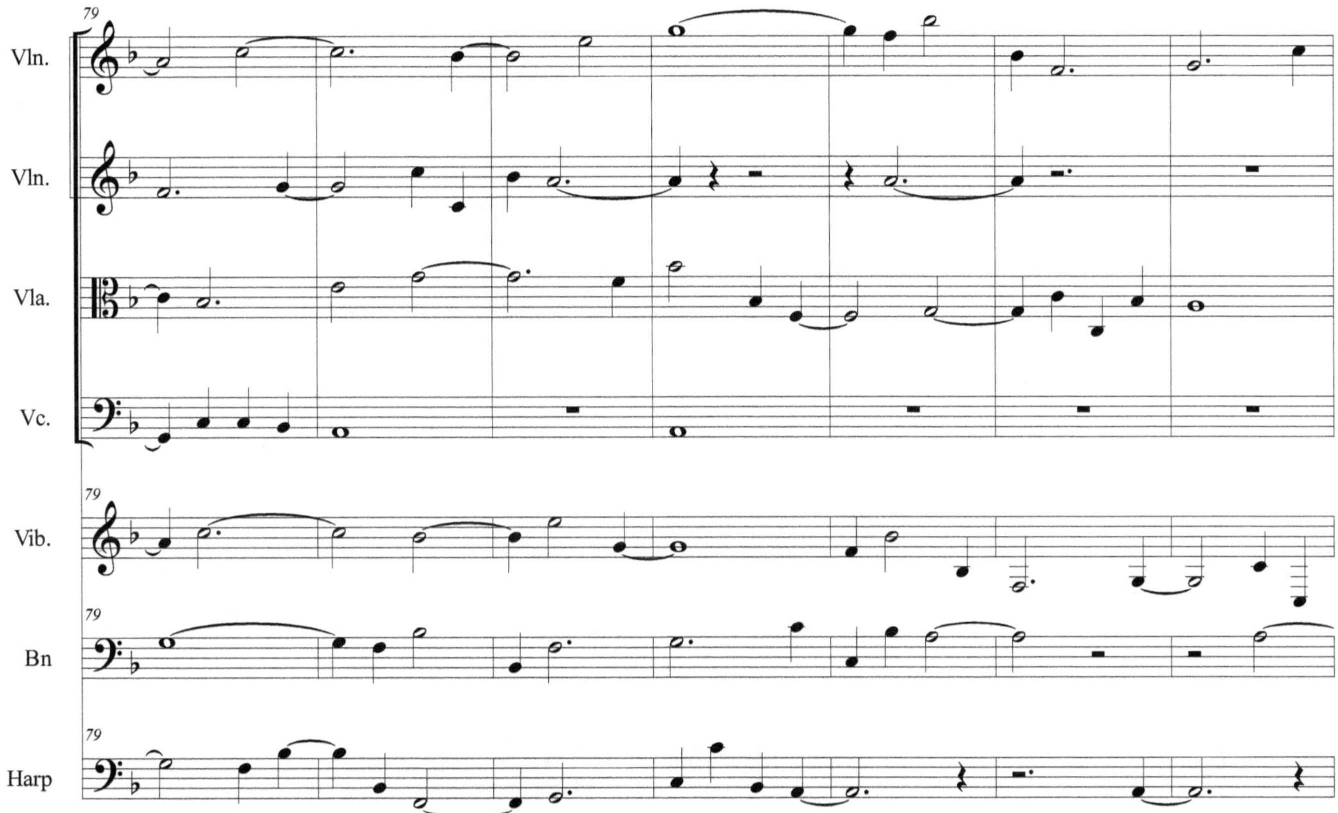
79
Vln.
Vln.
Vla.
Vc.
79
Vib.
79
Bn
79
Harp

π

18

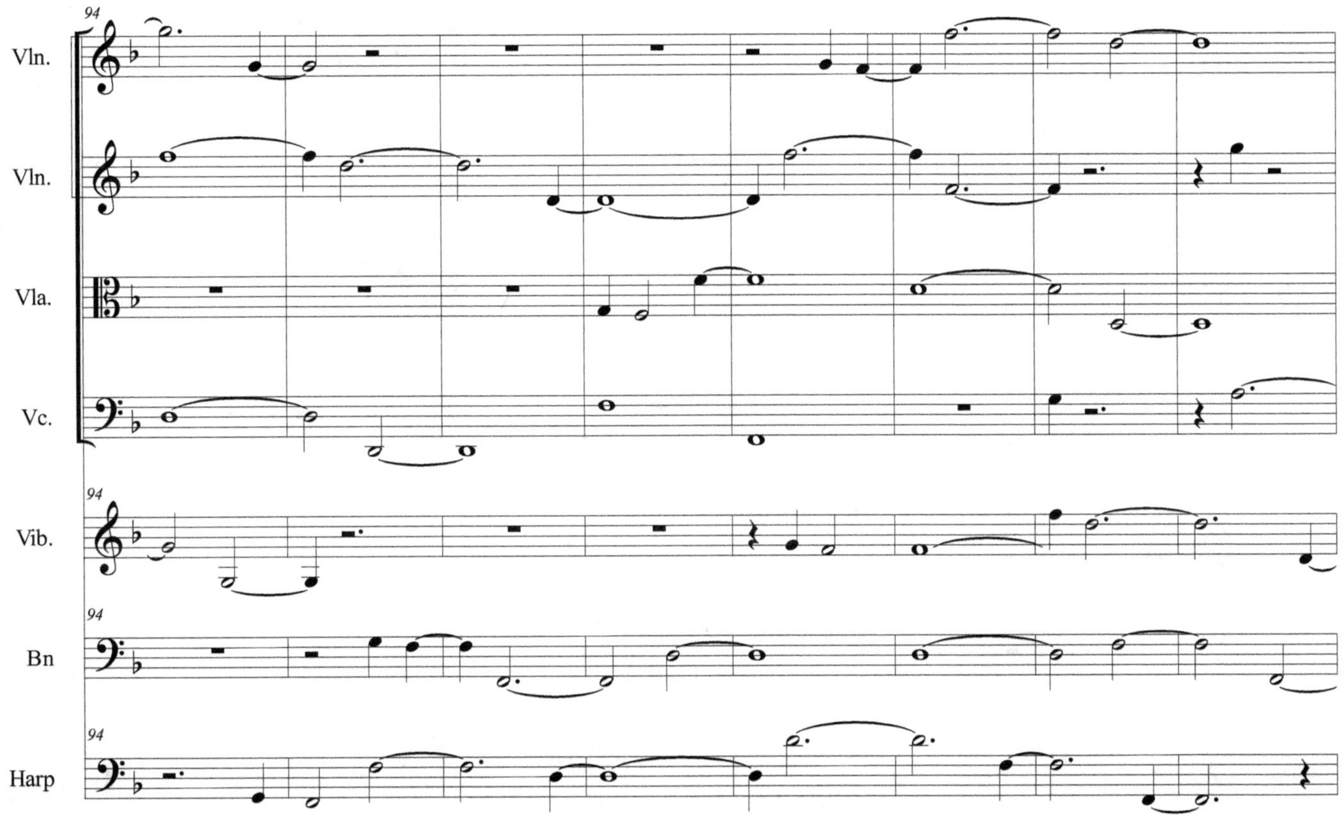
94
Vln.
Vln.
Vla.
Vc.
94
Vib.
94
Bn
94
Harp

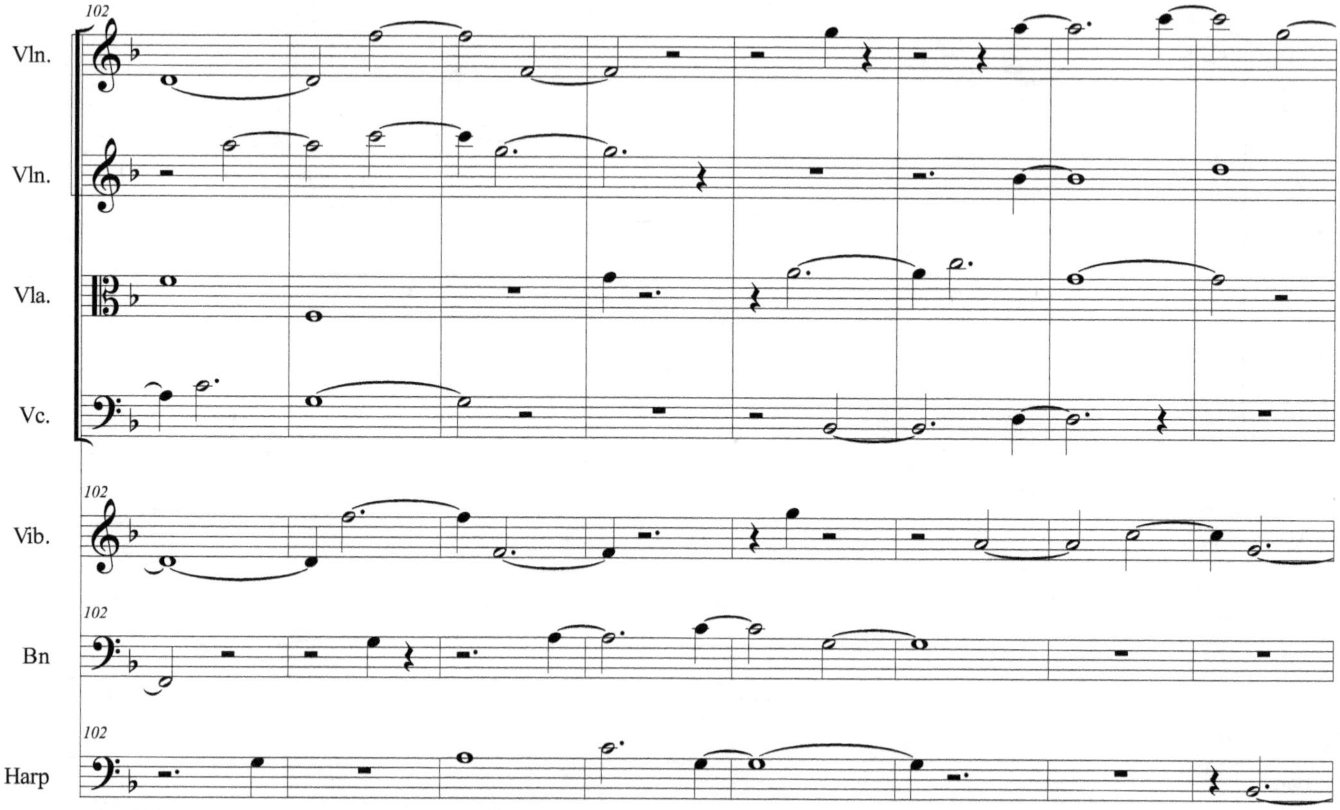
102
Vln.
Vln.
Vla.
Vc.
102
Vib.
102
Bn
102
Harp

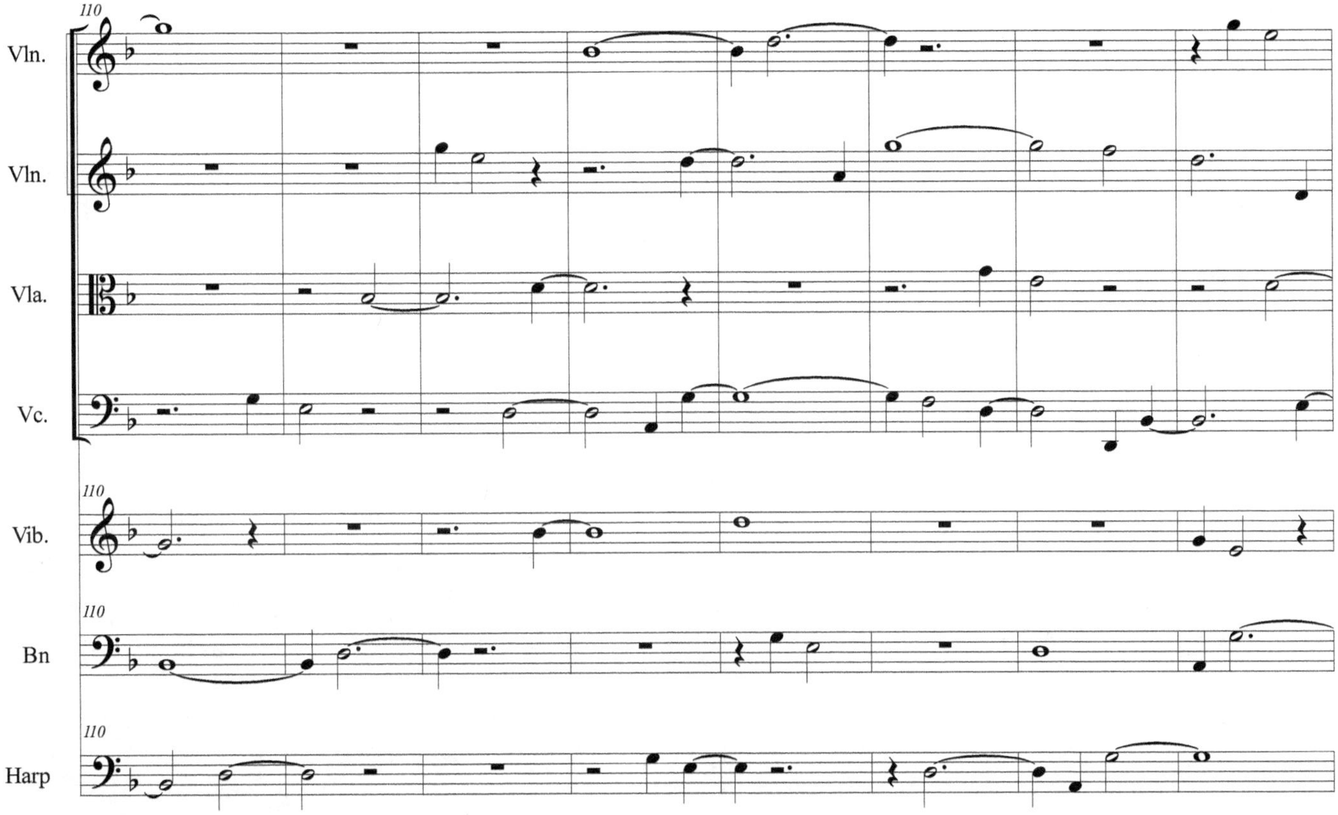
110
Vln.
Vln.
Vla.
Vc.
110
Vib.
110
Bn
110
Harp

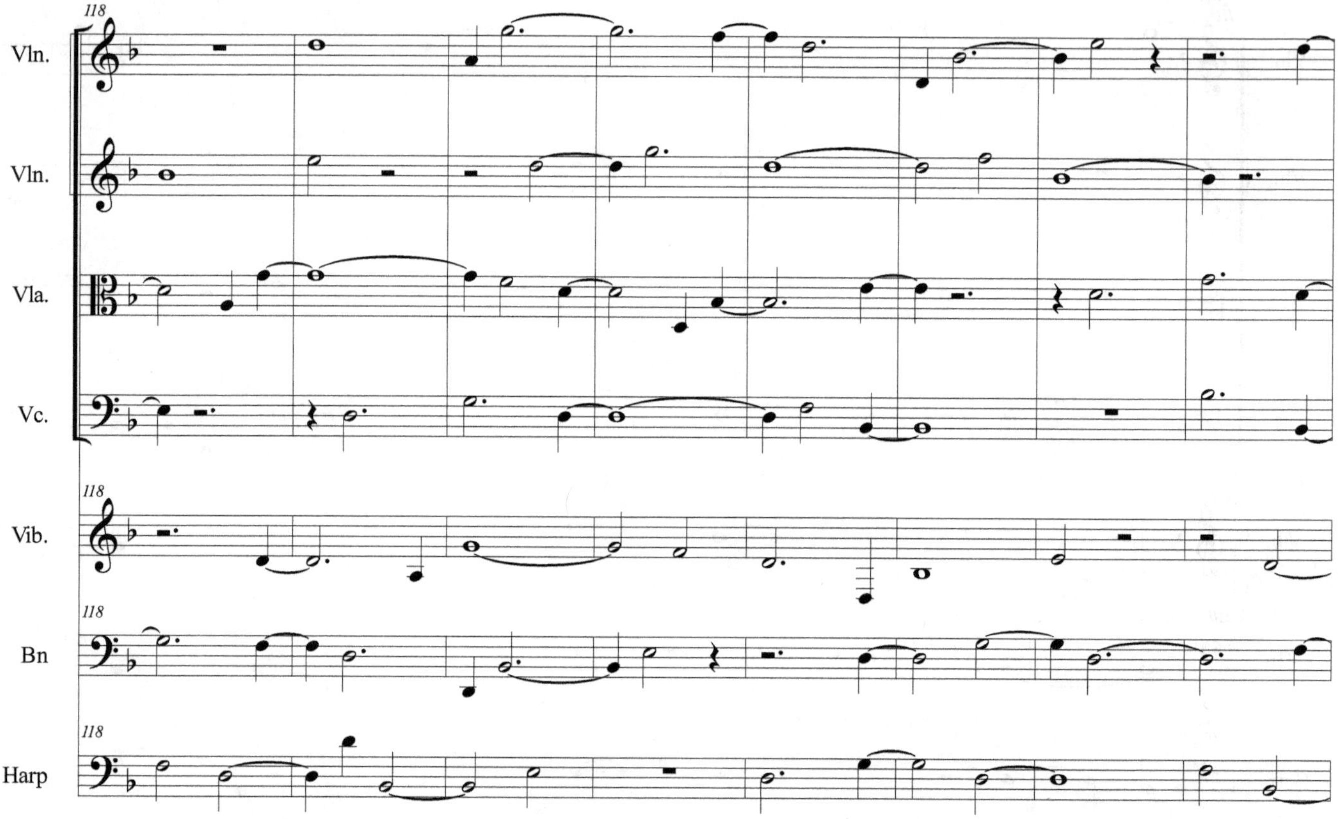
118
Vln.
Vln.
Vla.
Vc.
118
Vib.
118
Bn
118
Harp

23

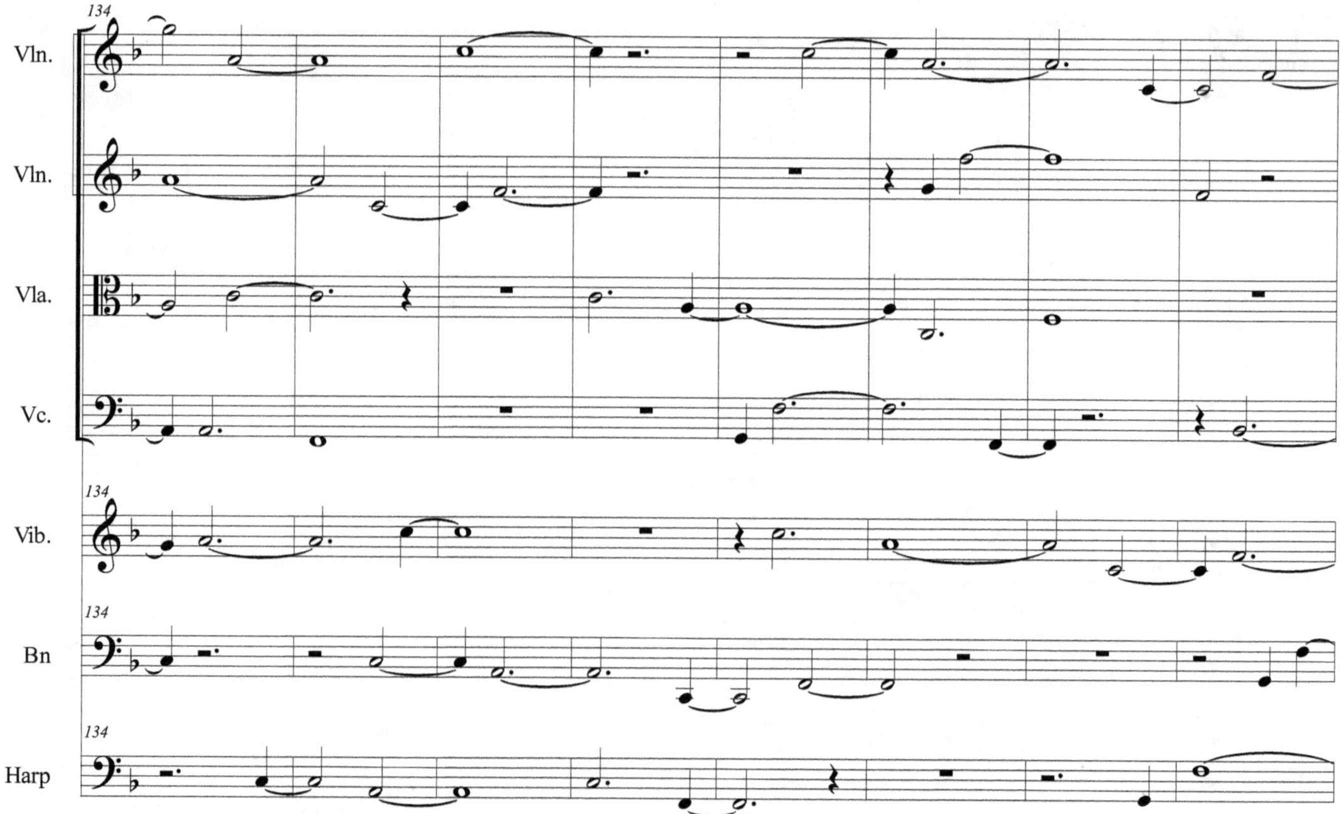
134
Vln.
Vln.
Vla.
Vc.
134
Vib.
134
Bn
134
Harp

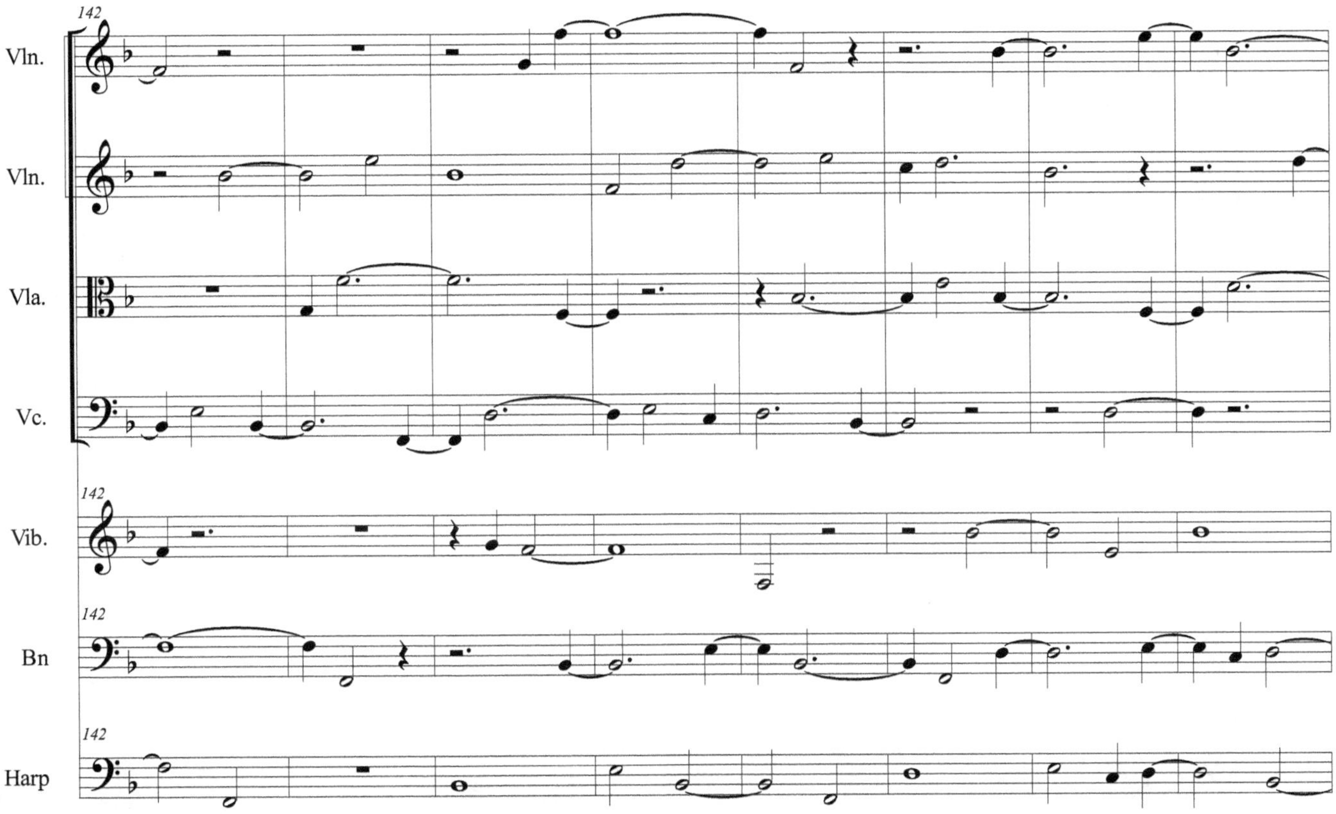
142
Vln.
Vln.
Vla.
Vc.
142
Vib.
142
Bn
142
Harp

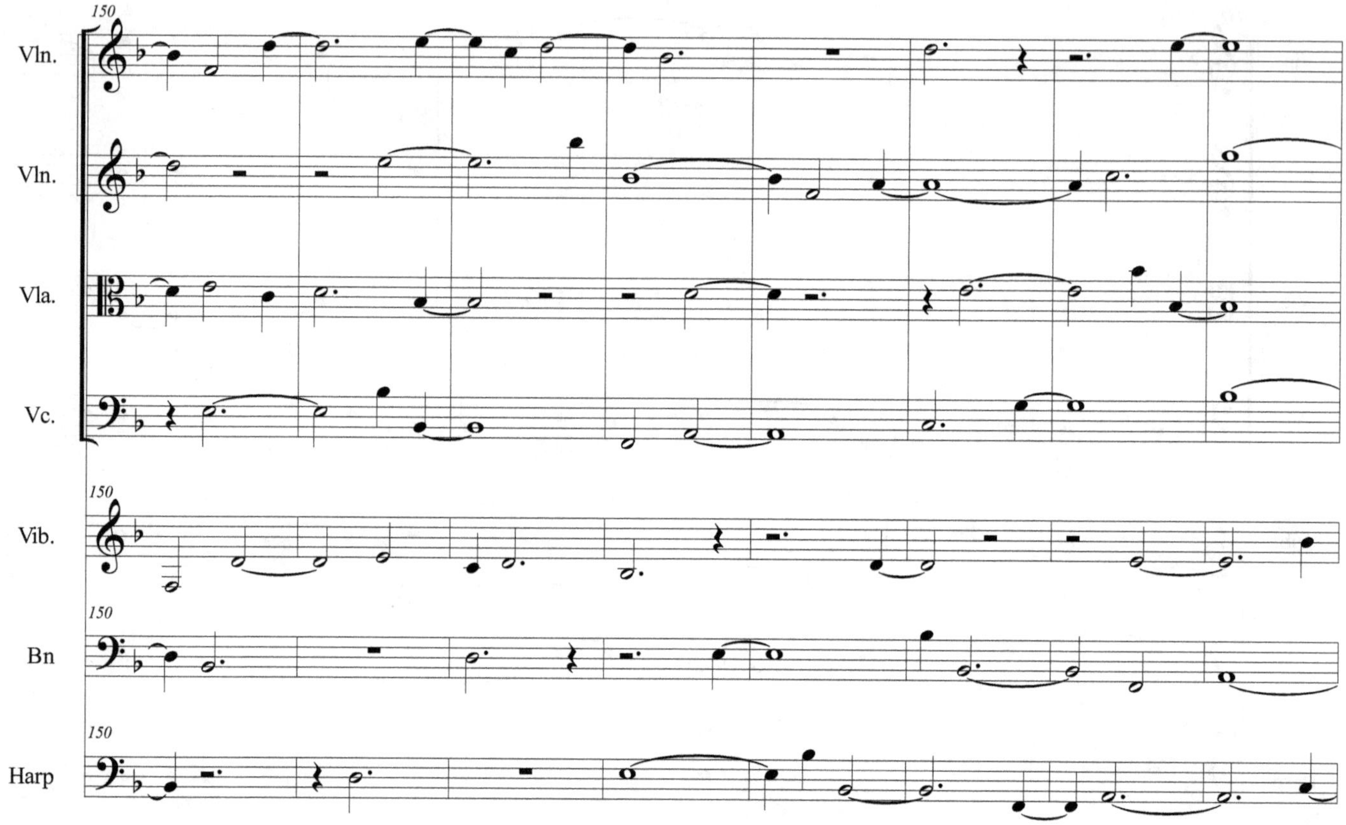
150
Vln.
Vln.
Vla.
Vc.
150
Vib.
150
Bn
150
Harp

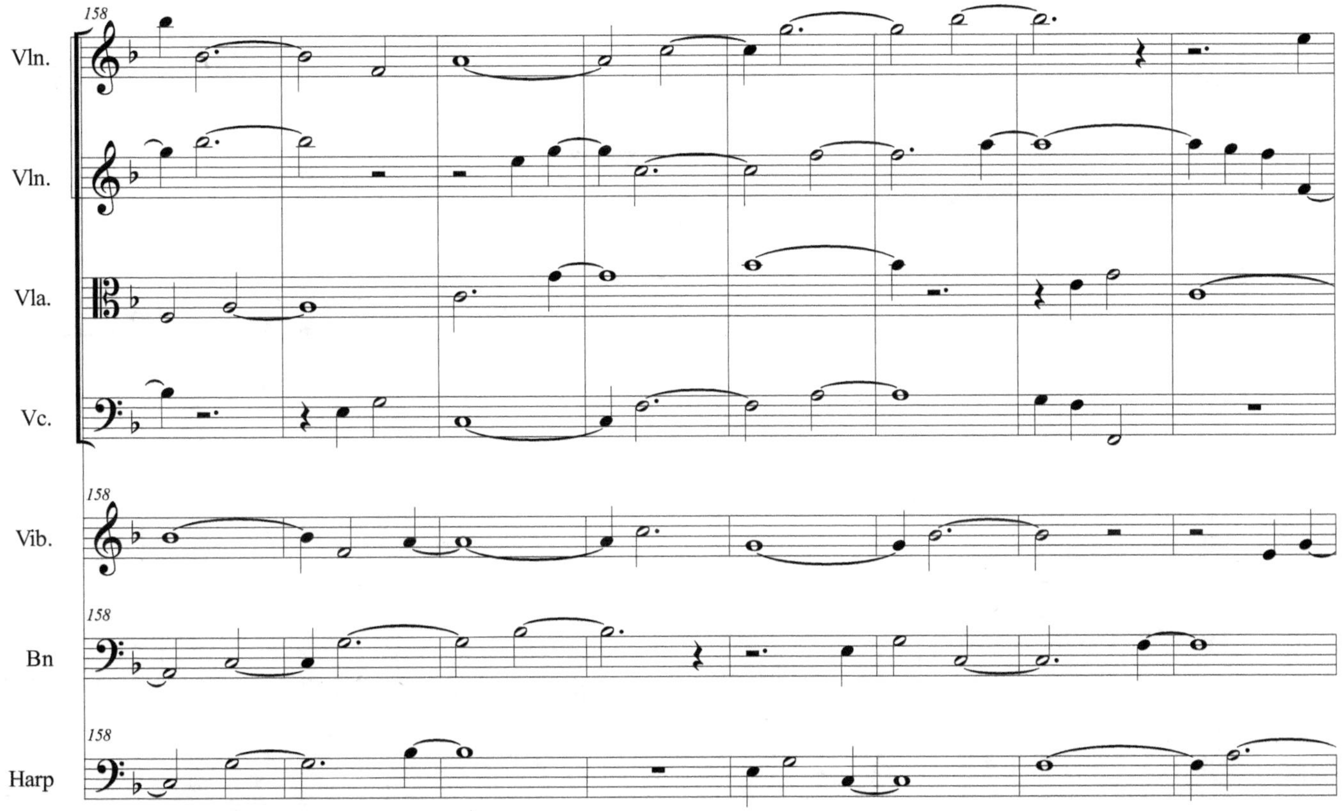
158
Vln.
Vln.
Vla.
Vc.
158
Vib.
158
Bn
158
Harp

π

28

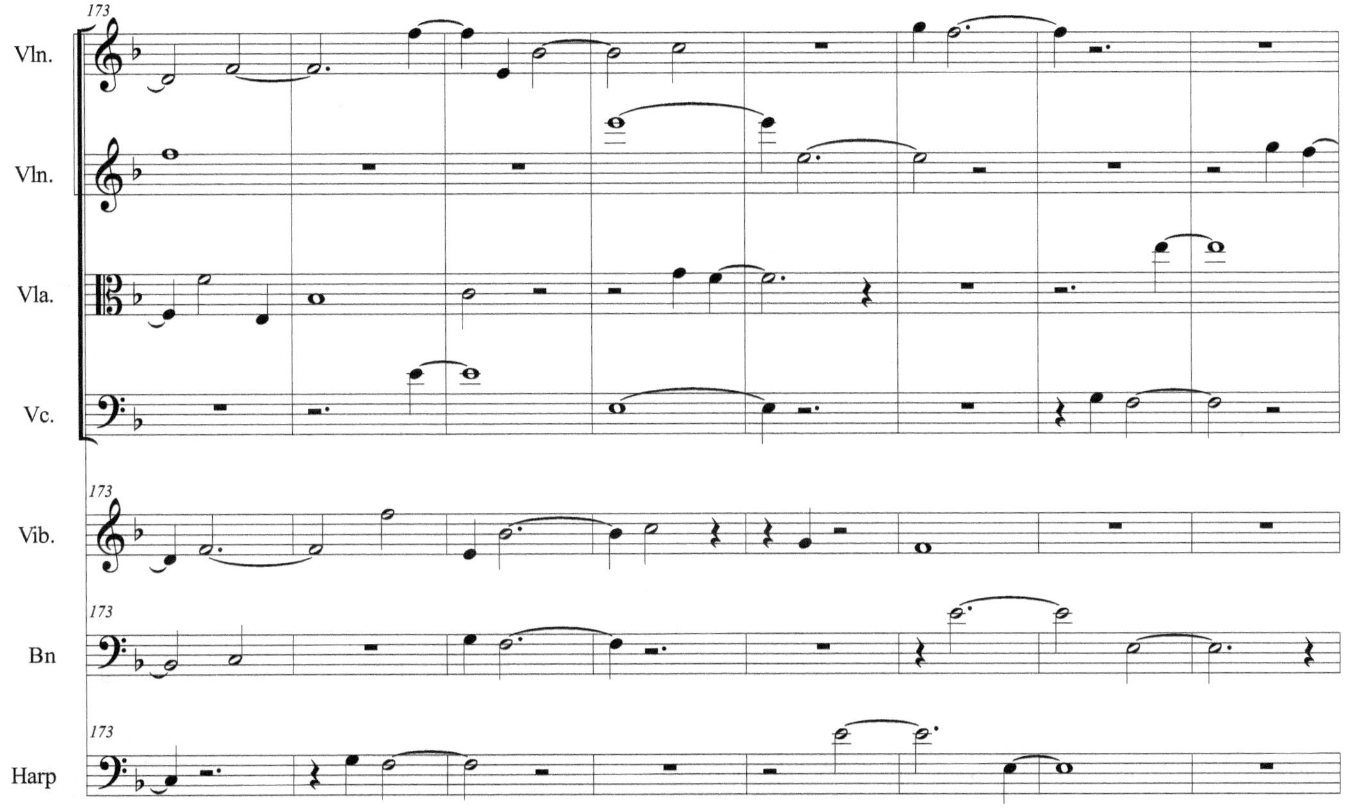
173
Vln.
Vln.
Vla.
Vc.
173
Vib.
173
Bn
173
Harp

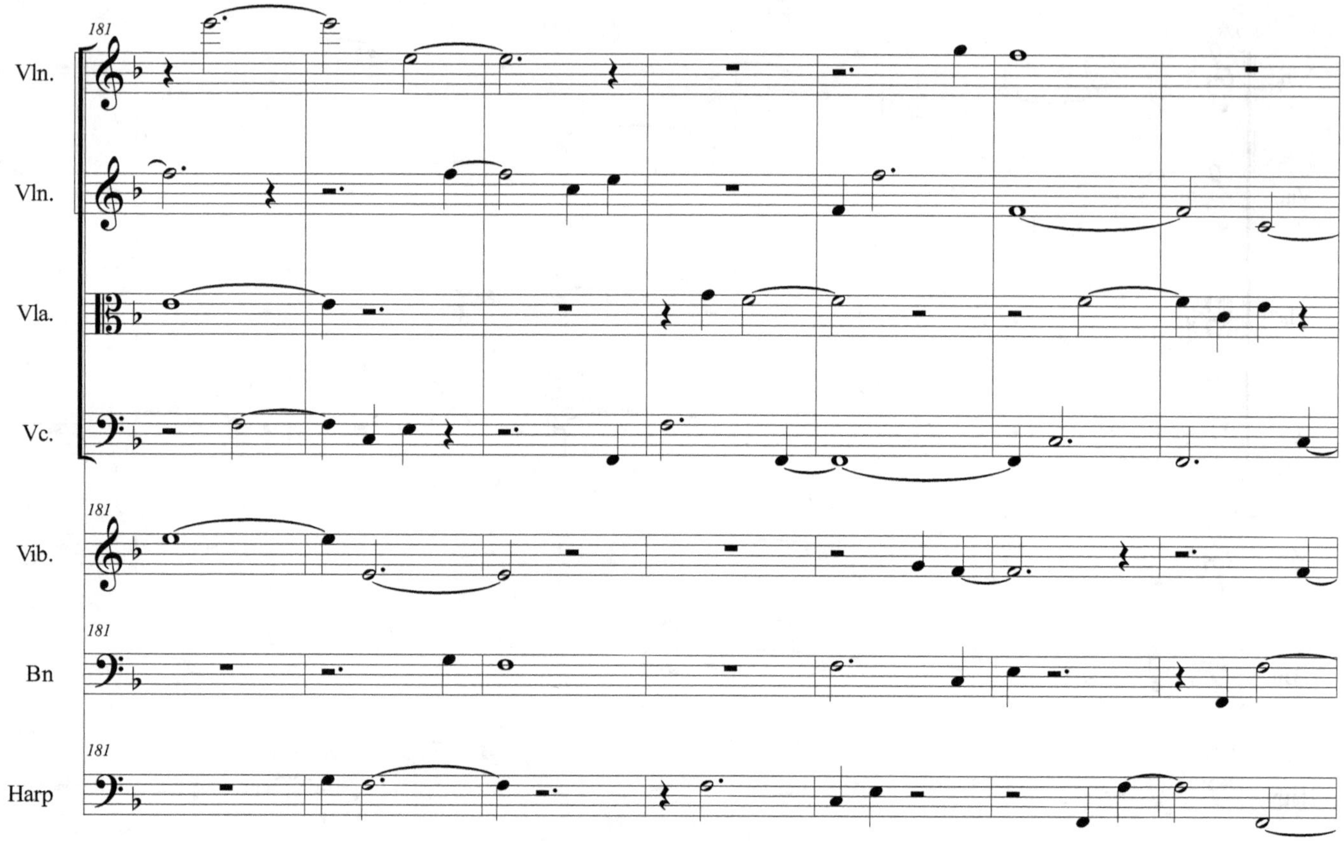
181
Vln.
Vln.
Vla.
Vc.
181
Vib.
181
Bn
181
Harp

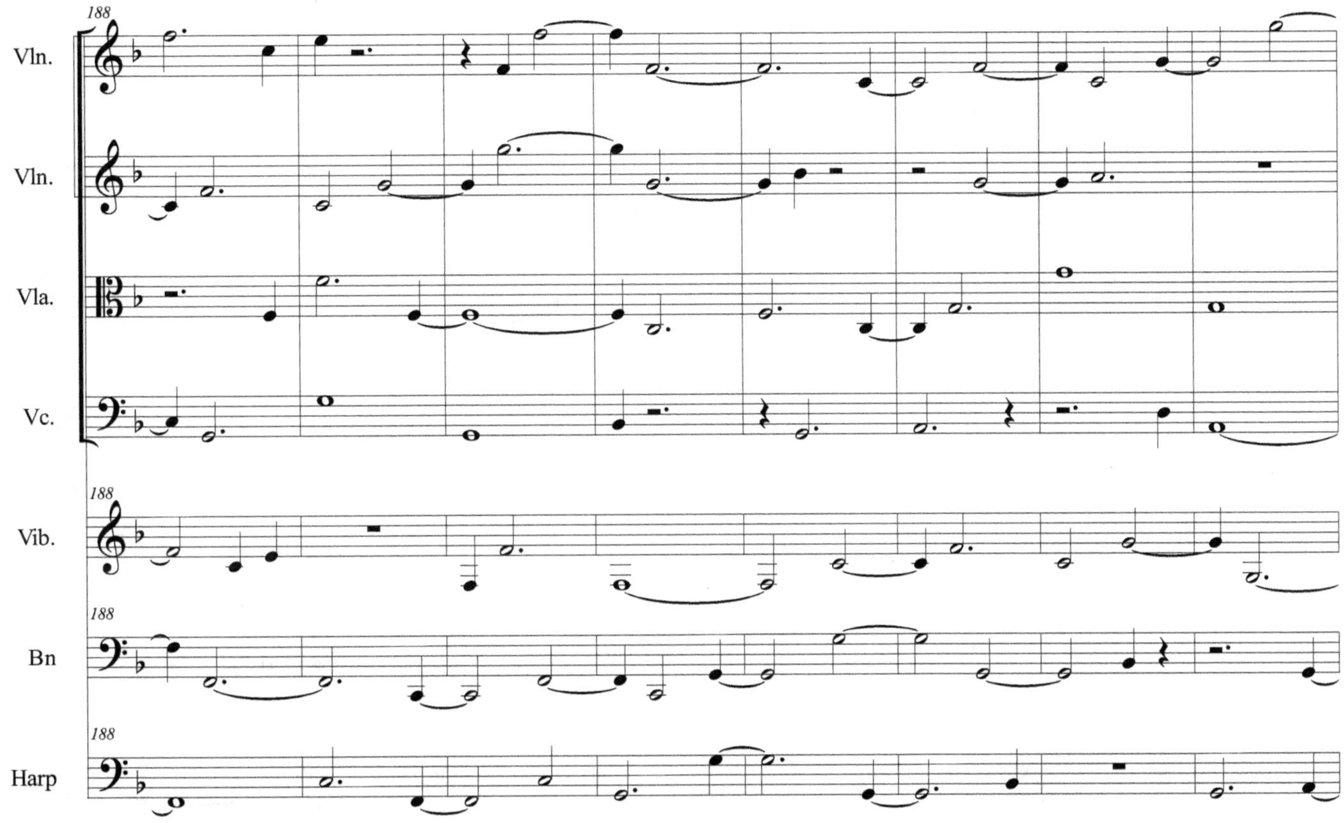
188
Vln.
Vln.
Vla.
Vc.
188
Vib.
188
Bn
188
Harp

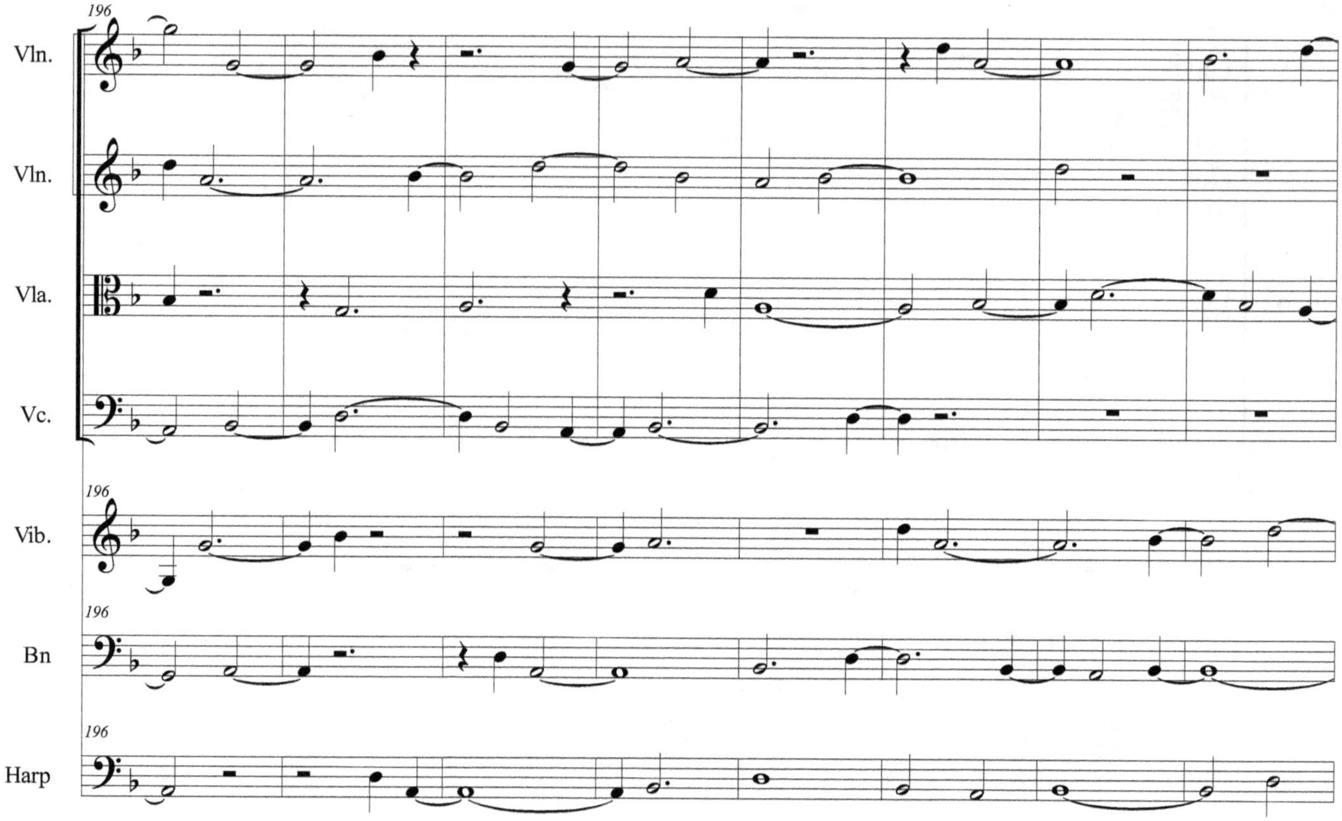
196
Vln.
Vln.
Vla.
Vc.
196
Vib.
196
Bn
196
Harp

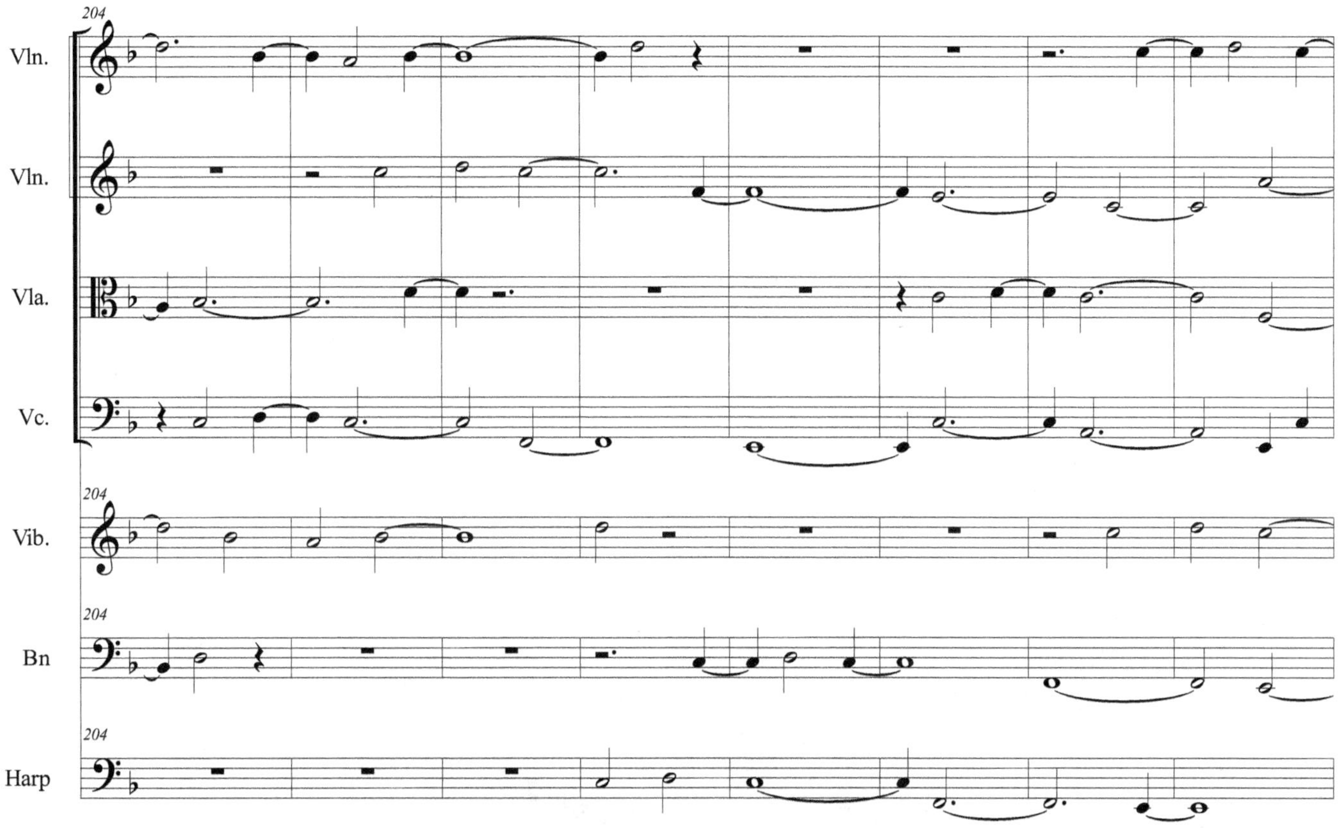
204
Vln.
Vln.
Vla.
Vc.
204
Vib.
204
Bn
204
Harp

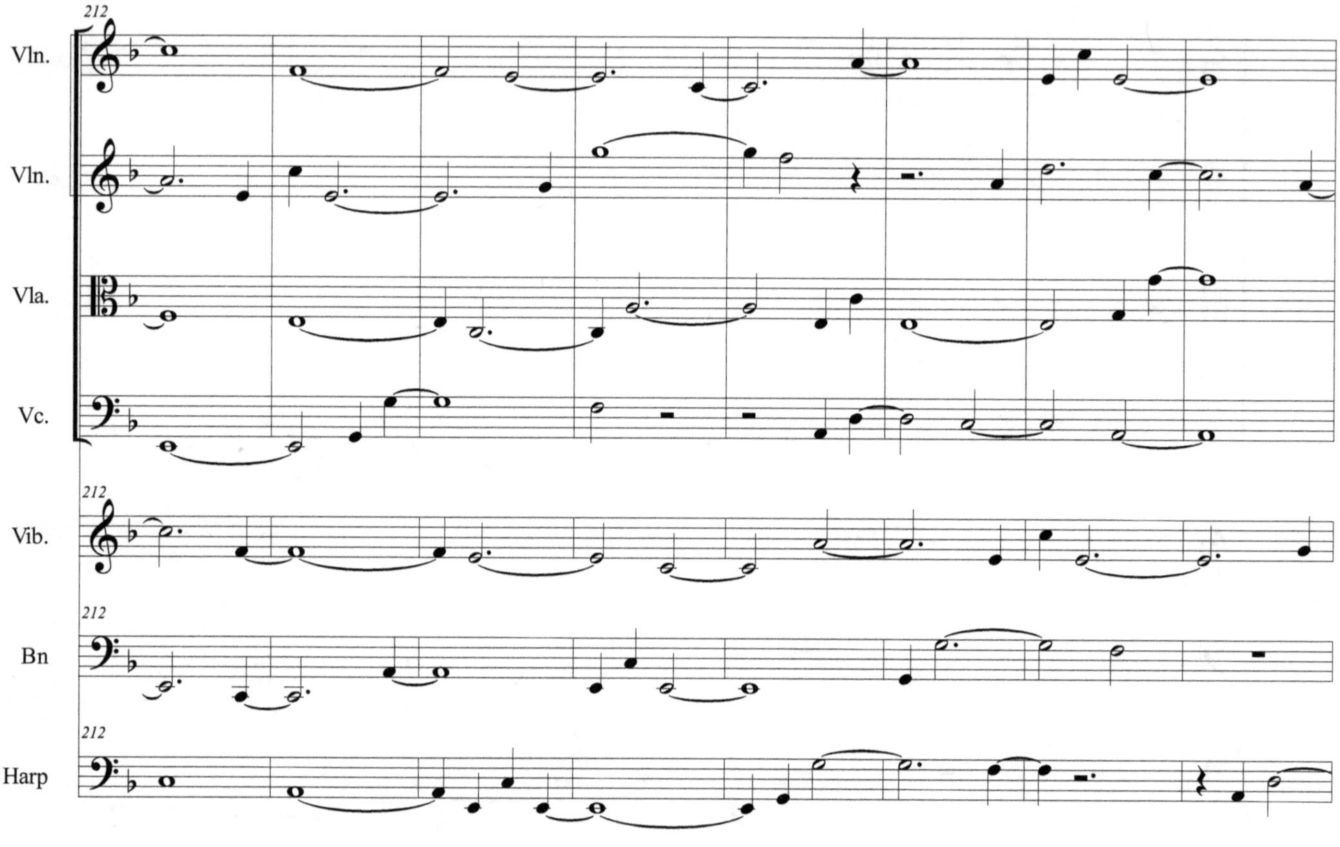
212
Vln.
Vln.
Vla.
Vc.
212
Vib.
212
Bn
212
Harp

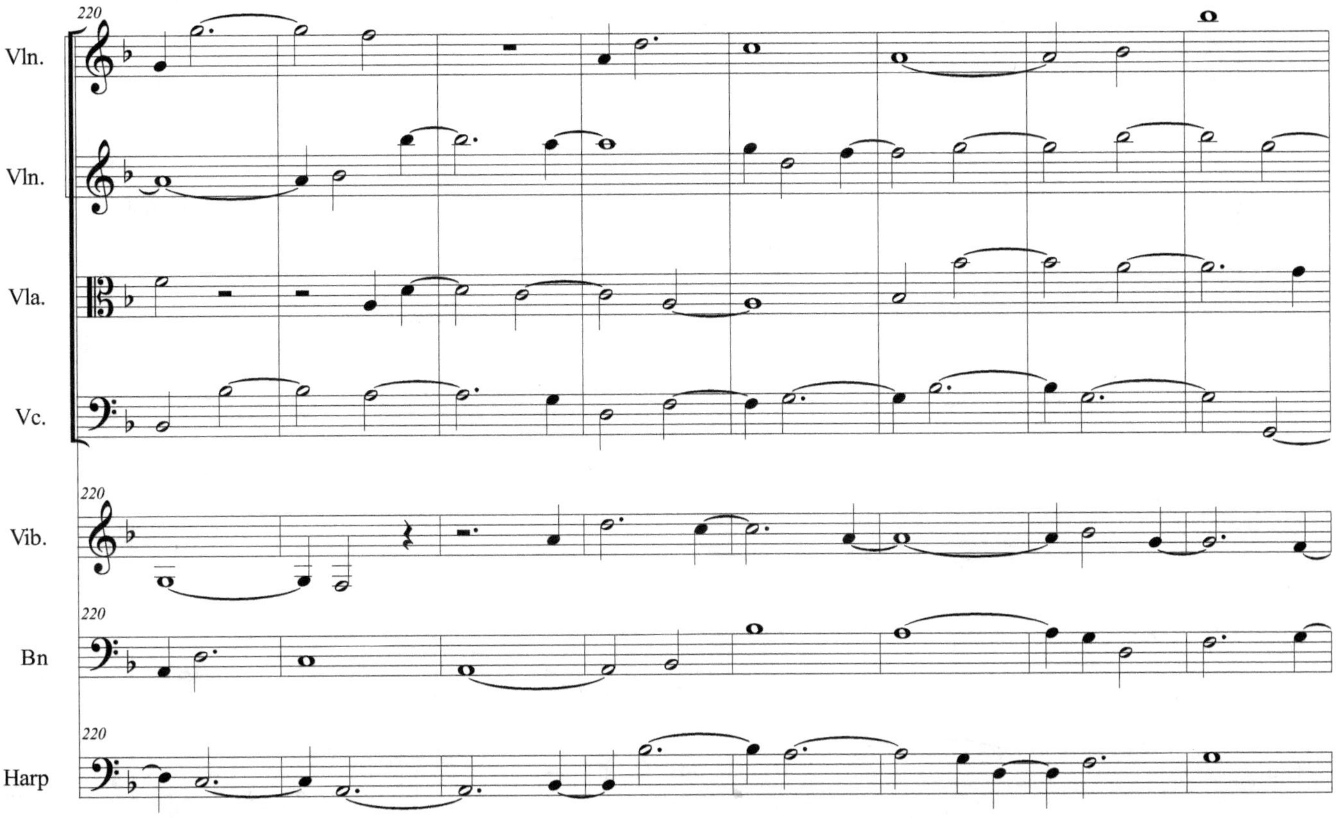
220
Vln.
Vln.
Vla.
Vc.
220
Vib.
220
Bn
220
Harp

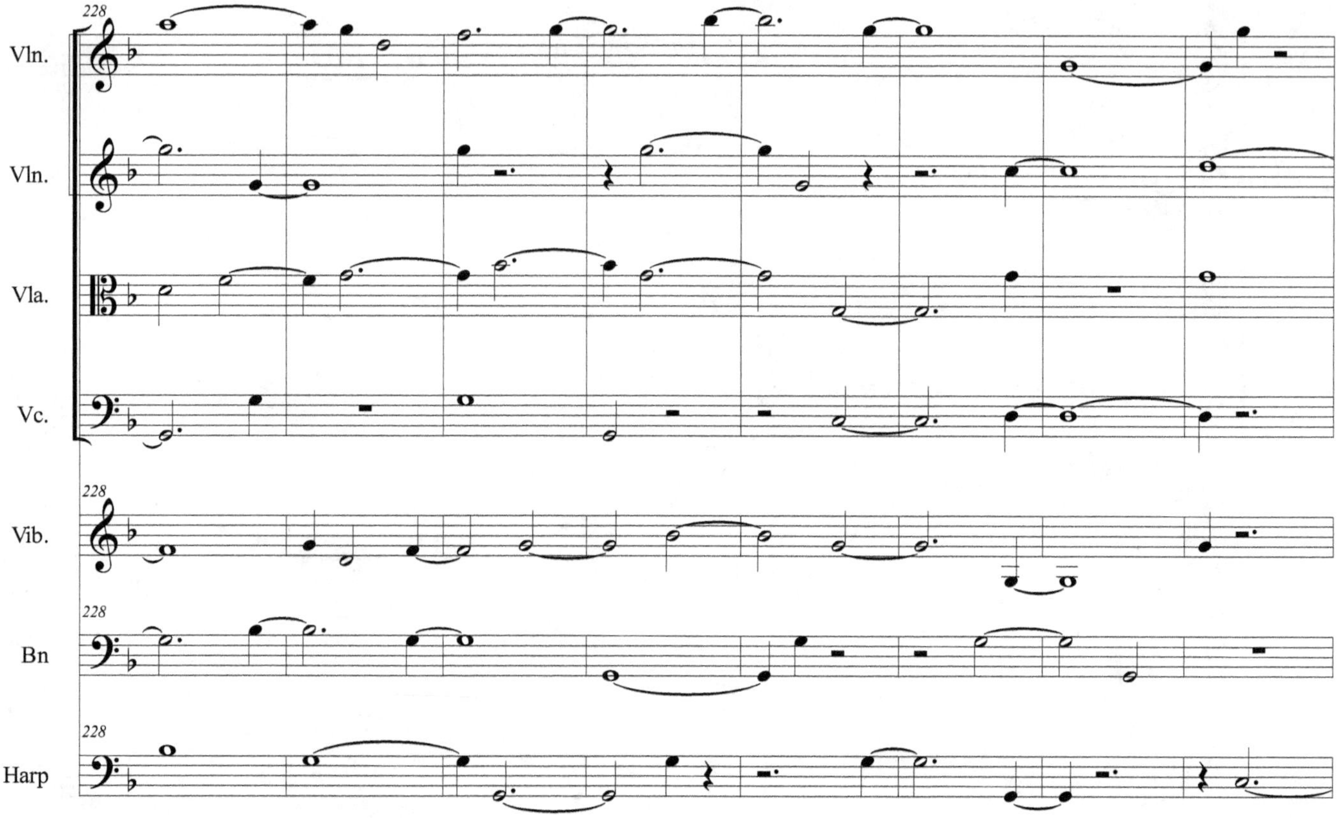
228
Vln.
Vln.
Vla.
Vc.
228
Vib.
228
Bn
228
Harp

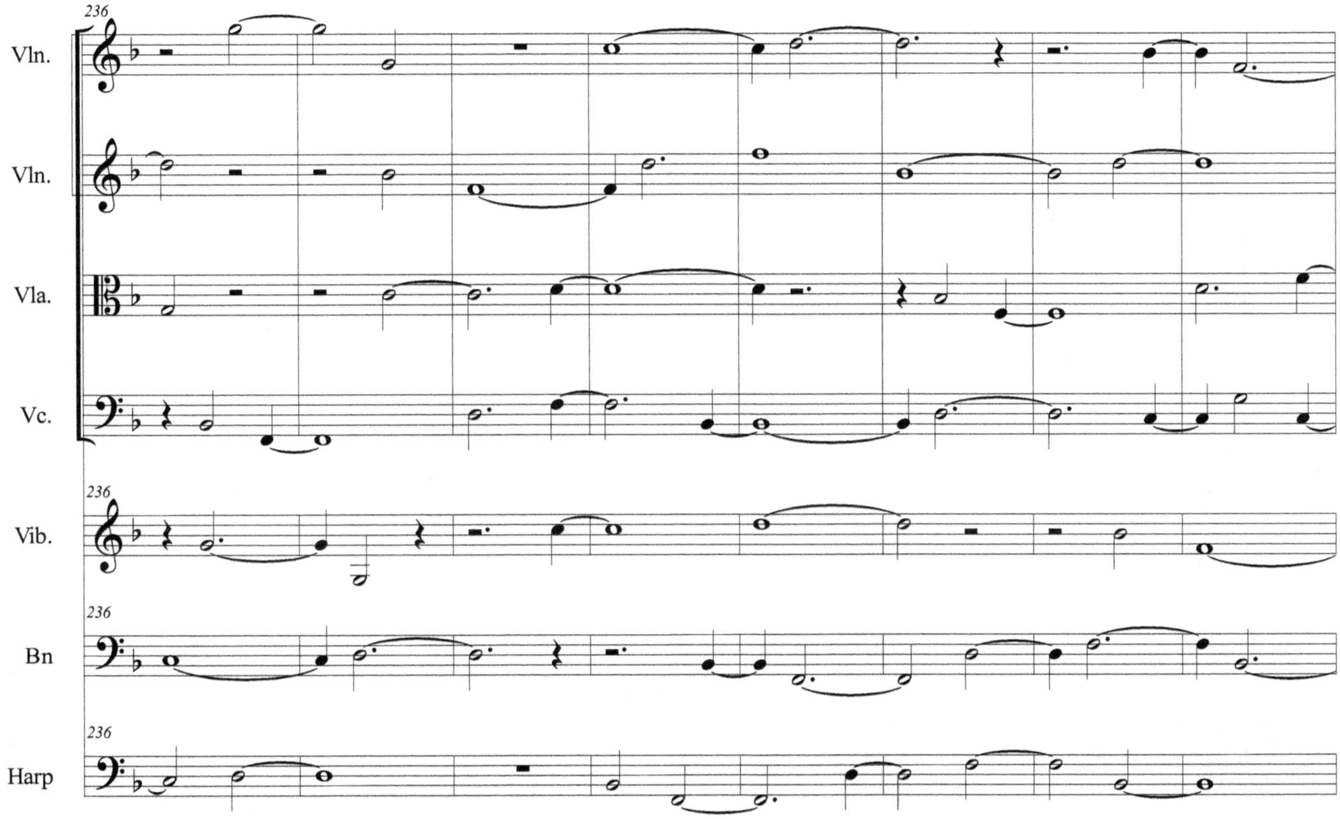
236
Vln.
Vln.
Vla.
Vc.
236
Vib.
236
Bn
236
Harp

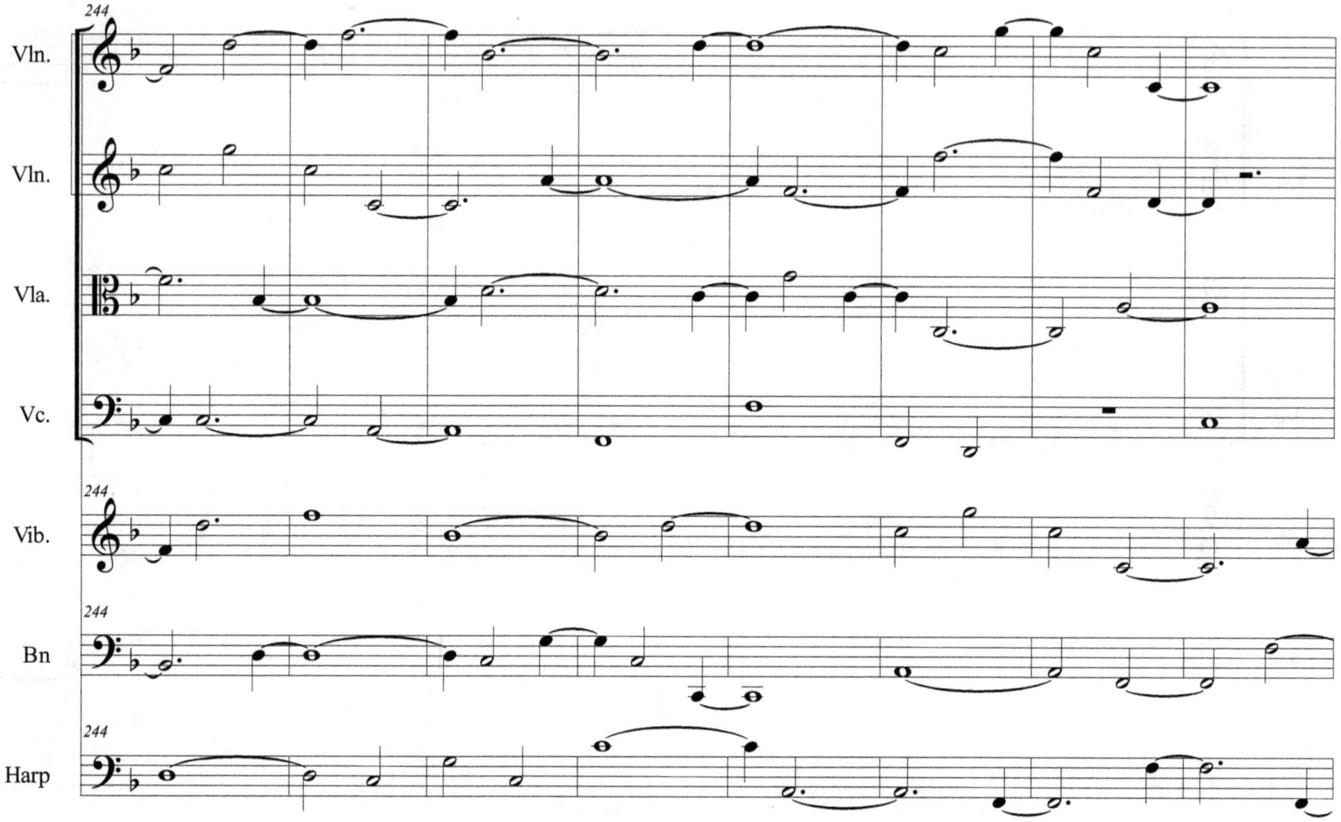
244
Vln.
Vln.
Vla.
Vc.
244
Vib.
244
Bn
244
Harp

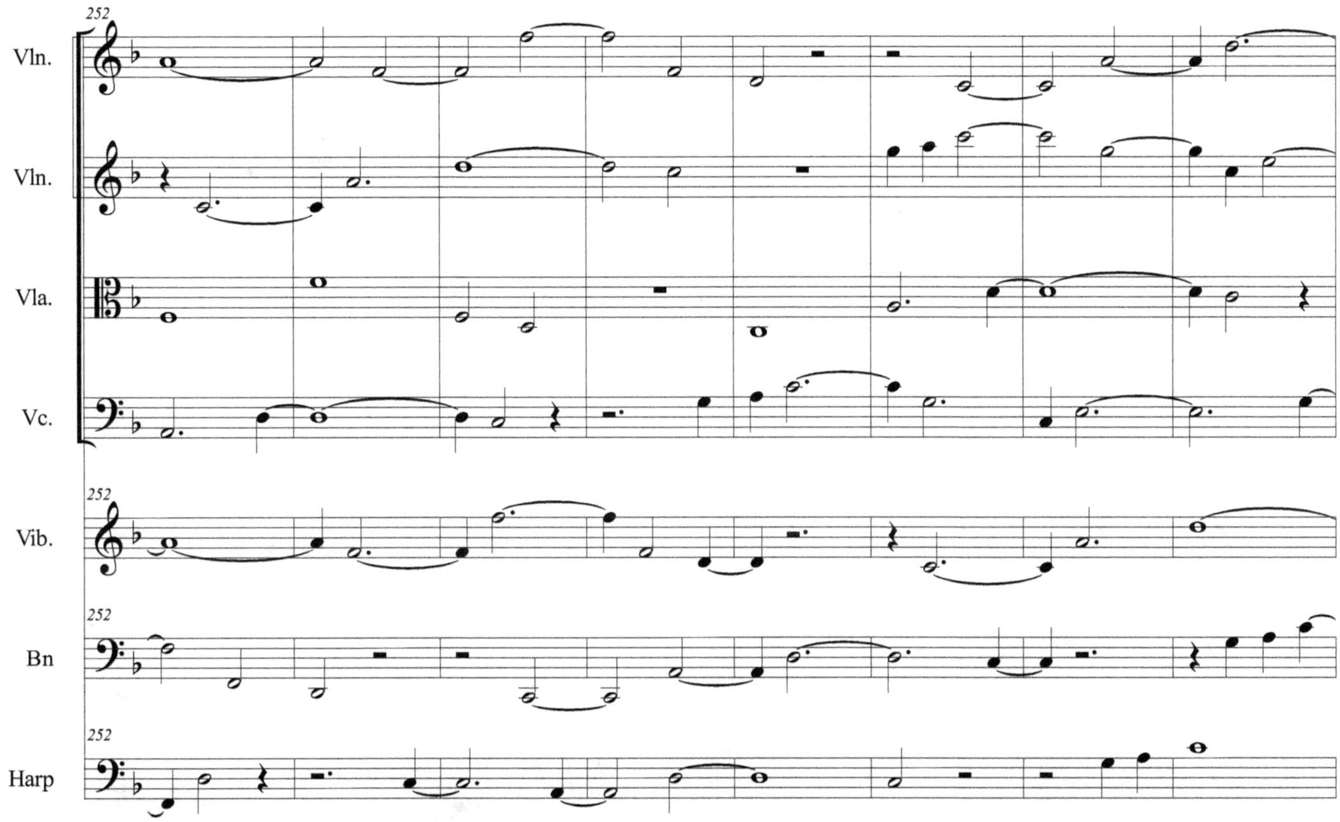
252
Vln.
Vln.
Vla.
Vc.
252
Vib.
252
Bn
252
Harp

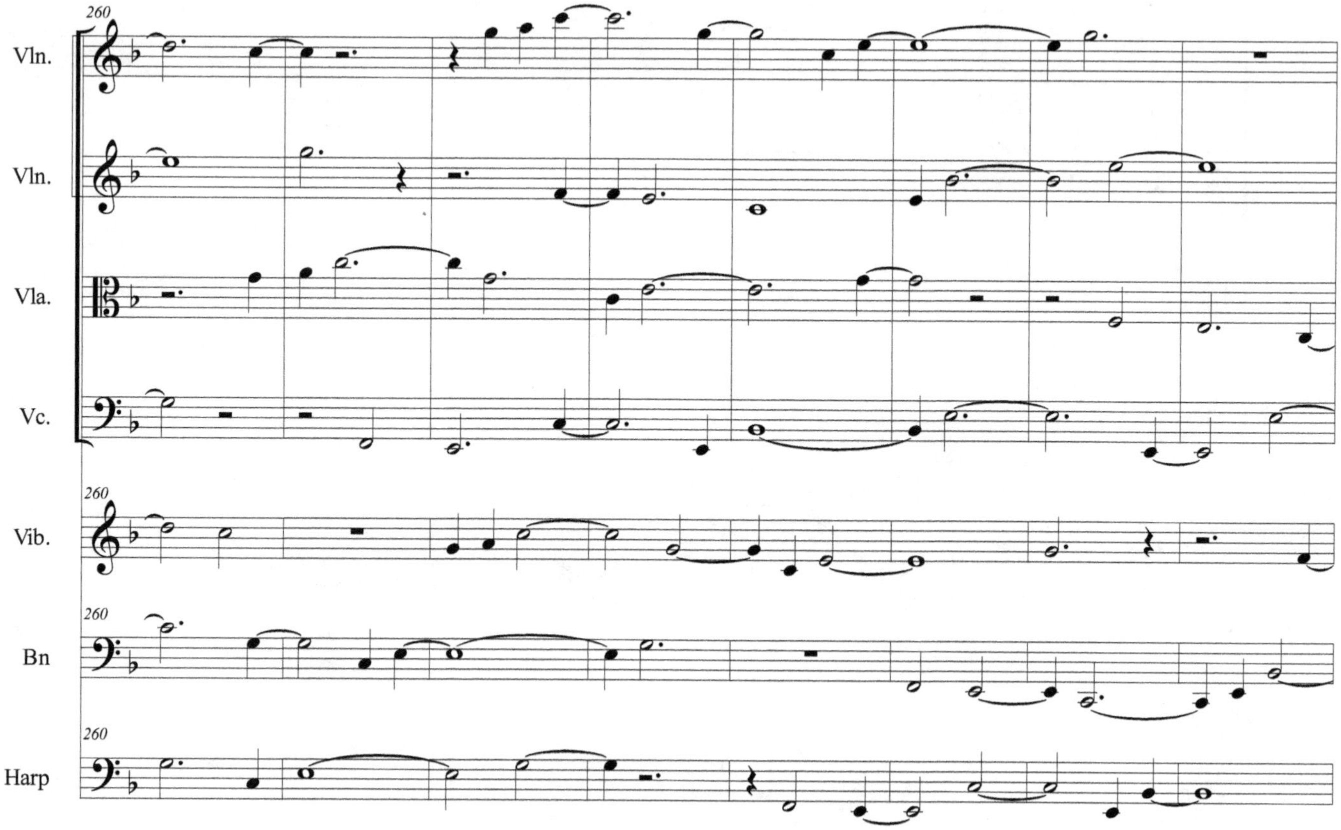
260
Vln.
Vln.
Vla.
Vc.
260
Vib.
260
Bn
260
Harp

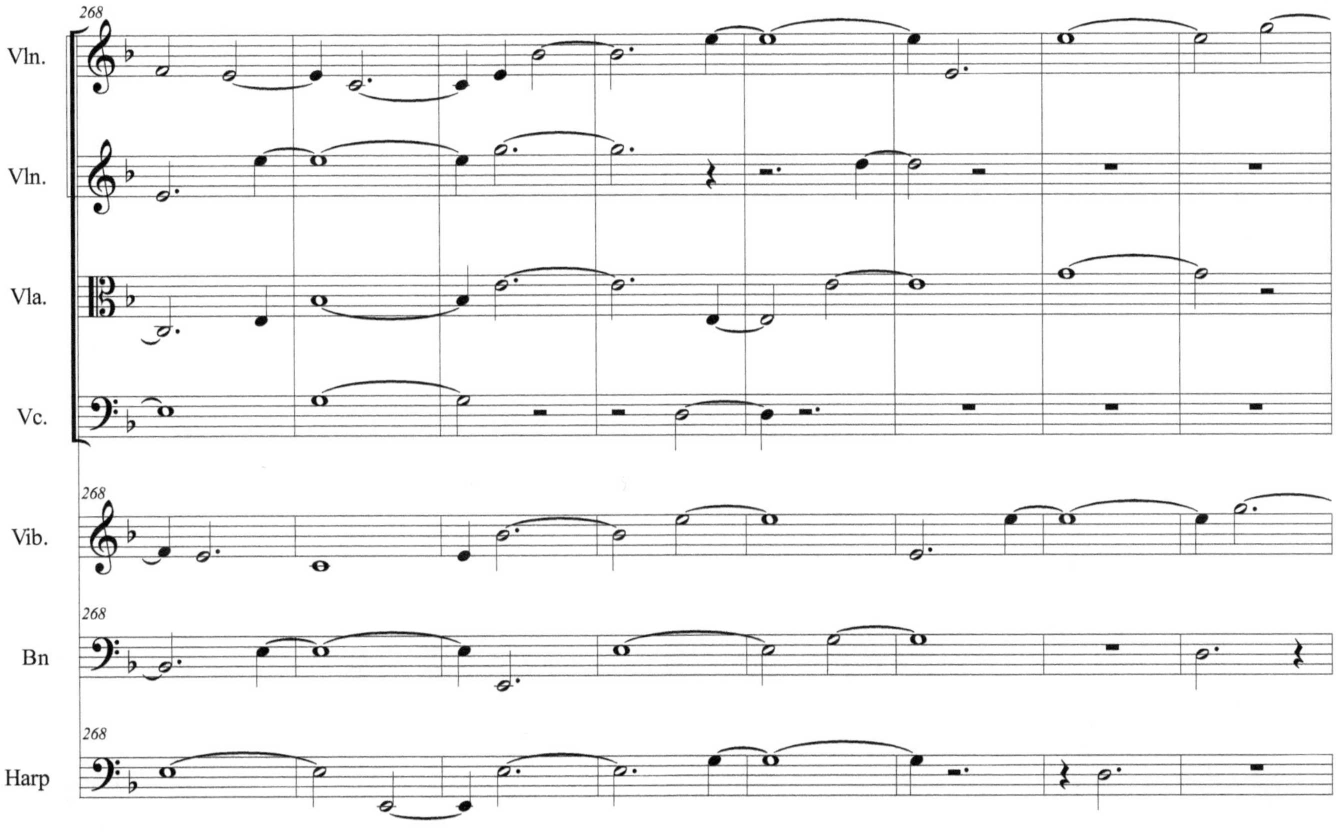
268
Vln.
Vln.
Vla.
Vc.
268
Vib.
268
Bn
268
Harp

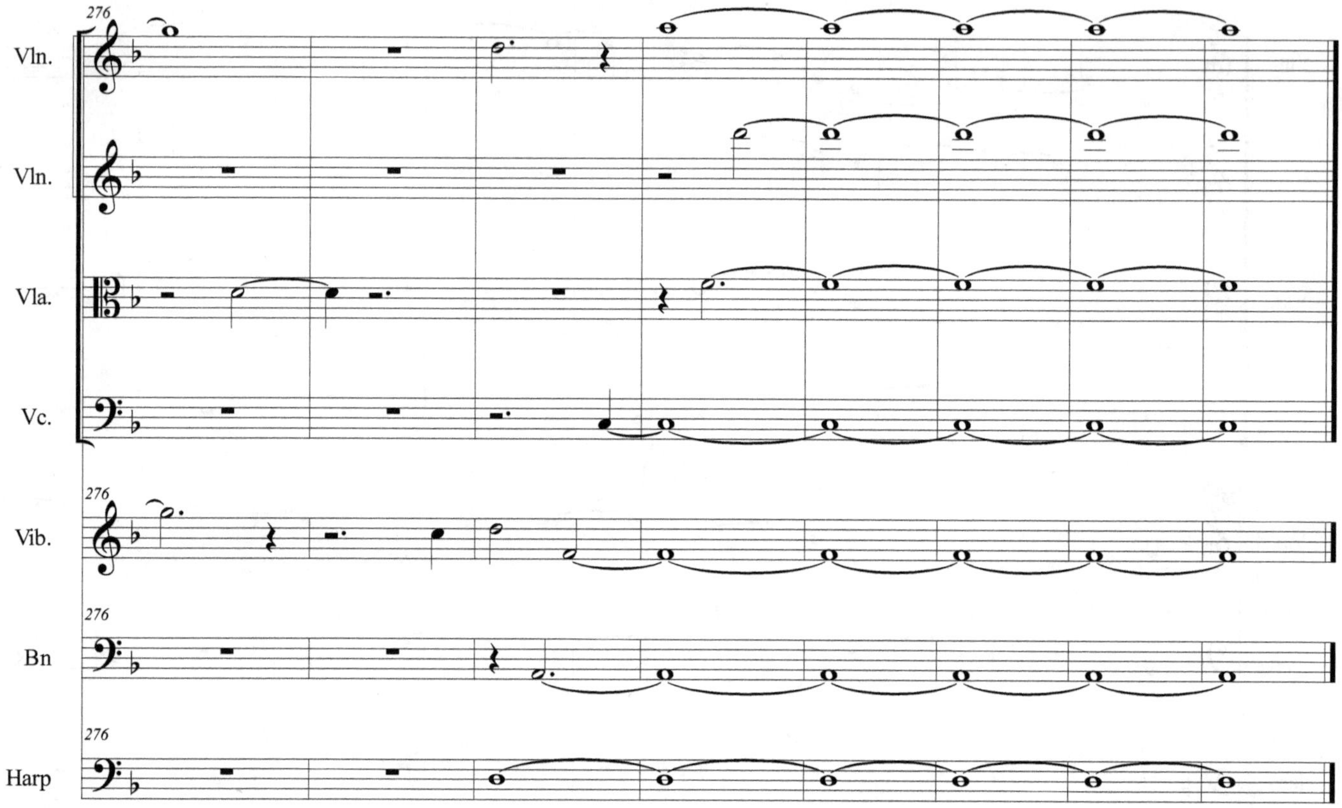
276
Vln.
Vln.
Vla.
Vc.
Vib.
Bn
Harp

Appendix

```
3.
1103755242 1026430215 1423063050 5600670163 2112201116 : 50
0210514763 0720020273 7246166116 3310450512 0207461615 : 100
0023357371 2431547464 7220615460 1260515574 4574241564 : 150
7741152665 5524341105 7110266535 4611363754 3364230413 : 200
5151433755 3260577727 1333640153 3755734341 5376655211 : 250
4772265647 6220213704 5437714444 5031450754 7105547560 : 300
4001745612 0543576026 3066444066 0705272346 4644261772 : 350
4375111475 3740662535 1075624353 3130343057 1526101025 : 400
2256717325 1220356045 5131553160 6065234452 7446002361 : 450
3506601062 4140413703 1220274430 5615547073 7071716713
```

The Working Number:

first few digits of π_7

3.06636514320361341102634022446522266435206502
40155443215426431025161154565220002622436103
30144323363101130410055004102412535211655210553
62515030331242424026100436305645305263302413
26140210045006340104466521000354000404111331
21523532354334540642646110025423321501311161114
53305035414420005262543124146150646366612503
40621566513342655053121614145360201046310465
24331422052601115466443004301420142342032404521
44151301324146205251661524433450450323500152
30030362164454610650213462563452443511056450
311105223325414...∞
```
```

FORMAL

Canon á 7

Cast in traditional 4/4 time

Diatonic scale, Dmin/Fmaj

About 19 min at quarternote=60

INSTRUMENTATION

Septet

Parts numerically assigned as:

0   violin

1   violin pizz.

2   viola

3   cello

4   vibraphone

5   bassoon

6   concert harp

DYNAMICS

Dynamics should center about *mp*, but much variation is permitted, and conductors should encourage players to "feel it".

PITCH

306_7 to base 10 = 313 → first 313 digits (of 306_7) to use as pitch template

30663651432036134110263402244652226643520650240155443215426431025161154565220002622436103301443233631011304100550041024125352116552105536251503033124242402610043630564530526330241326140210045006340104466521000354000404111331215235323543345406426461100254233215013111611145330503541442000526254312414615064636661125

Assign pitches to digits:

0=F, 1=G, 2=A, 3=Bb, 4=C, 5=D, 6=E

Yields this row of pitches:

BFEEBEDGCBAFBEGBCGGFAEBCFAACCEDA
AAEECBDAFEDFACFGDDCCBAGDCAECBGF
ADGEGGDCDEDAAFFFAEAACBEGFBBFGCC
BABBEBGFGGBFCGFFDDFFCGFACGADBDA
GGEDDAGFDDBEADGDFBFBBGACACACFAE
GFFCBEBFDECDBFDAEBBFACGBAEGCFAGF
FCDFFEBCFGFCCEEDAGFFFBDCFFFCFCGGG
BBGAGDABDBABDCBBCDCFECAECEGGFFA
DCABBAGDFGBGGGEGGGCDBBFDFBDCGC
CAFFFDAEADCBGACGCEGDFECEBEEGAD

NOTE DURATIONS

0=4 beat tacet; *establishes segments to facilitate phrasing*

1   1 beat (quarter note)

2   2 beats

3   3 beats

…

6   6 beats

To derive durations for each note in the canon, I have made a retrograde sequence of the numerical string I used for deriving pitches (see **PITCH***):*

52166636460516414213452625000244145305033541 1
16111310512332452001164624604543345323532512 1
33111404000453000125664401043600540012041623 1
42033625035465036340016204242133030515263 55
01255611253521420140055001403110136332344103 3
01634226200022565451161520134624512344551042 0
56025346622256442204362011431630234156366 03

CREATION OF THE CANON MELODY

By pairing each number in the above sequence with each number in the row of pitches generated in a previous section (**PITCH**), the melody of the canon has been generated. This table is presented at the end of this section.

PART ENTRANCE ORDER

Initial occurrence of <u>unique</u> digits in order of appearance in π_7, corresponding to instrument assignment:
30663**651**4**3****2** → 3065142

Order of entrance is therefore:

3   clarinet
0   violin
6   double bass
5   bassoon
1   flute
4   cello
2   harpsichord

PART ENTRANCE TIMES

Initial occurrence of <u>non-zero</u> digits (zero would mean entering at 0 beats after previous part's entry) in order of appearance in

π_7: <u>**30663651**</u> → 3663651

Pairing 3663651 with the **PART ENTRANCE ORDER** *generated above yields:*

clarinet	Enters (to begin the work) at Measure1/Beat3
violin	Enters **6** beats later at M3/B1
double bass	Enters **6** beats later at M4/B3
bassoon	Enters **3** beats later at M5/B2
flute	Enters **6** beats later at M6/B4
cello	Enters **5** beats later at M8/B1
harpsichord	Enters **1** beat later at M8/B2

CANON MELODY

Column one is pitch; column two is duration in beats;
0 value in duration column indicates a 4-beat rest.

Bb	5	F	3	D	0
F	2	A	4	A	3
E	1	E	5	F	3
E	6	Bb	2	E	5
Bb	6	C	6	D	4
E	6	F	2	F	1
D	3	A	5	A	1
G	6	A	0	C	1
C	4	C	0	F	6
Bb	6	C	0	G	1
A	0	E	2	D	1
F	5	D	4	D	1
Bb	1	A	4	C	3
E	6	A	1	C	1
G	4	A	4	Bb	0
Bb	1	E	5	A	5
C	4	E	3	G	1
G	2	C	0	D	2
G	1	Bb	5	C	3

A	3	A	5	F	4
E	2	E	3	G	5
C	4	A	2	G	3
Bb	5	A	3	Bb	0
G	2	C	5	F	0
F	0	Bb	3	C	0
A	0	E	2	G	1
D	1	G	5	F	2
G	1	F	1	F	5
E	6	Bb	2	D	6
G	4	Bb	1	D	6
G	6	F	3	F	4
D	2	G	3	F	4
C	4	C	1	C	0
D	6	C	1	G	1
E	0	Bb	1	F	0
D	4	A	4	A	4
A	5	Bb	0	C	3
A	4	Bb	4	G	6
F	3	E	0	A	0
F	3	Bb	0	D	0
F	4	G	0	Bb	5

D	4		Bb	5		D	3
A	0		G	4		Bb	3
G	0		A	6		F	0
G	1		C	5		D	3
E	2		A	0		A	0
D	0		C	3		E	5
D	4		A	6		Bb	1
A	1		C	3		Bb	5
G	6		F	4		F	2
F	2		A	0		A	6
D	3		E	0		C	3
D	1		G	1		G	5
Bb	4		F	6		Bb	5
E	2		F	2		A	0
A	0		C	0		E	1
D	3		Bb	4		G	2
G	3		E	2		C	5
D	6		Bb	4		F	5
F	2		F	2		A	6
Bb	5		D	4		G	1
F	0		E	2		F	1
Bb	3		C	1		F	2

C	5	C	0	D	2
D	3	F	1	C	0
F	5	F	3	Bb	0
F	2	F	6	Bb	0
E	1	C	3	C	2
Bb	4	F	3	D	2
C	2	C	2	C	5
F	0	G	3	F	6
G	1	G	4	E	5
F	4	G	4	C	4
C	0	Bb	1	A	5
C	0	Bb	0	E	1
E	5	G	3	C	1
E	5	A	3	E	6
D	0	G	0	G	1
A	0	D	1	G	5
G	1	A	6	F	2
F	4	Bb	3	F	0
F	0	D	4	A	1
F	3	Bb	2	D	3
Bb	1	A	2	C	4
D	1	Bb	6	A	6

Bb	2	D	3	A	1
Bb	4	F	4	C	4
A	5	Bb	6	G	3
G	1	D	6	C	1
D	2	C	2	E	6
F	3	G	2	G	3
G	4	C	2	D	0
Bb	4	C	5	F	2
G	5	A	6	E	3
G	5	F	4	C	4
G	1	F	4	E	1
E	0	F	2	Bb	5
G	4	D	2	E	6
G	2	A	0	E	3
G	0	E	4	E	6
C	5	A	3	G	6
D	6	D	6	A	0
Bb	0	C	2	D	3
Bb	2	Bb	0		
F	5	G	1		

UPON REFLECTION...

for string orchestra

●

by

Gerald Brennan
© 2011

Upon reflection...

Gerald Brennan

Score

57

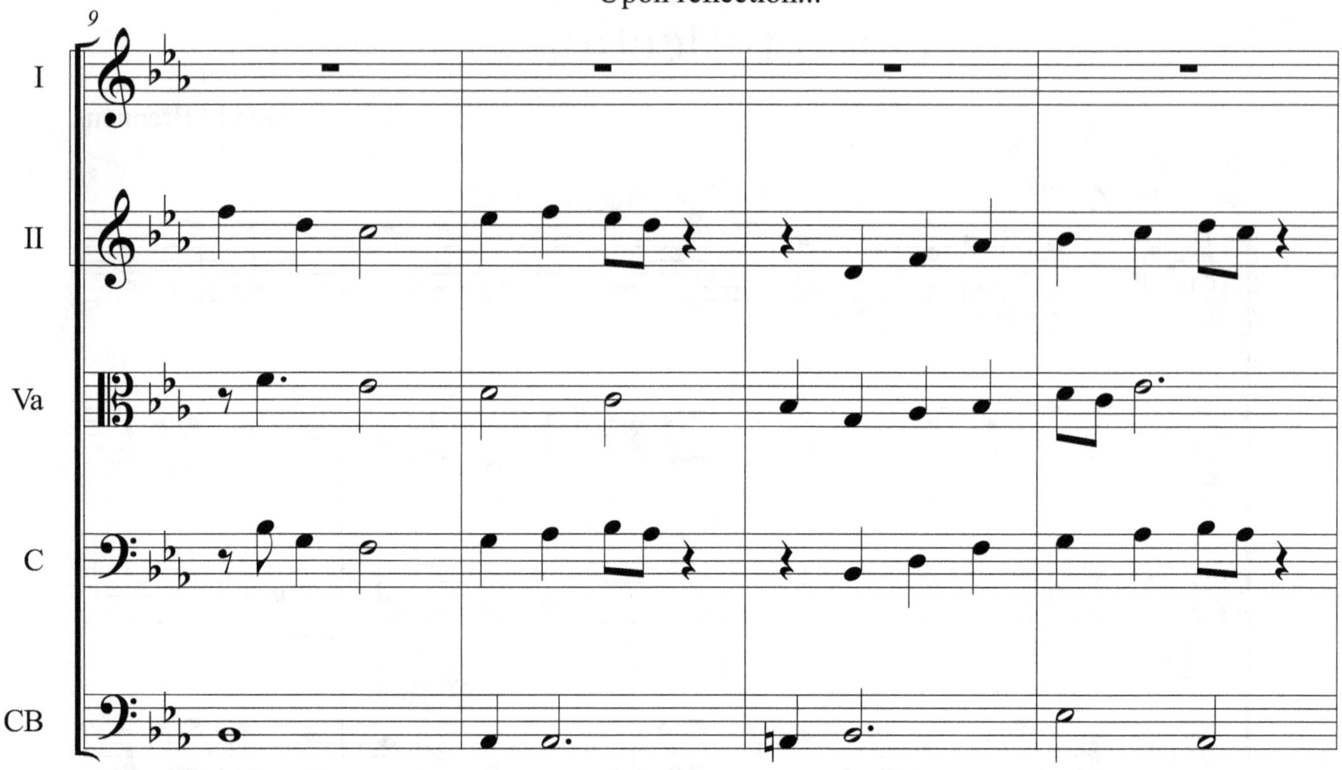
9
I
II
Va
C
CB

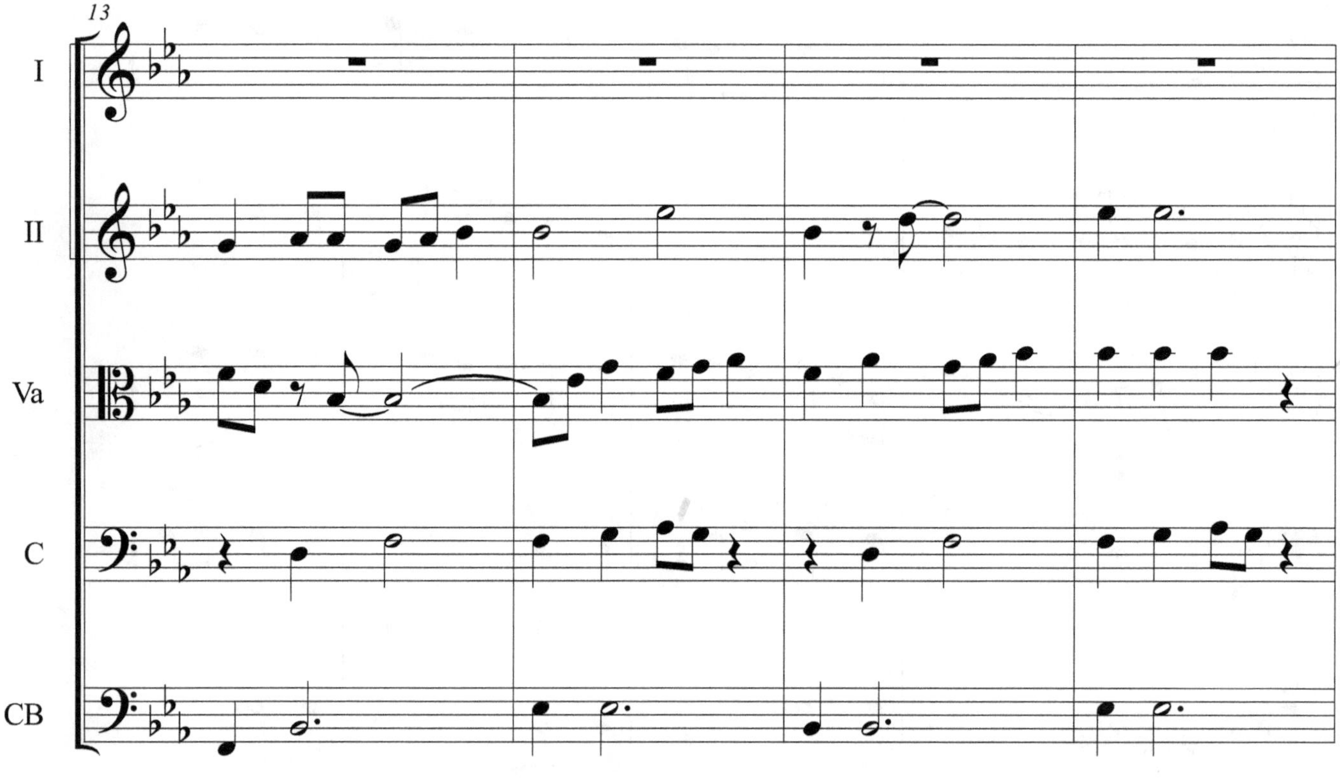
13
I
II
Va
C
CB

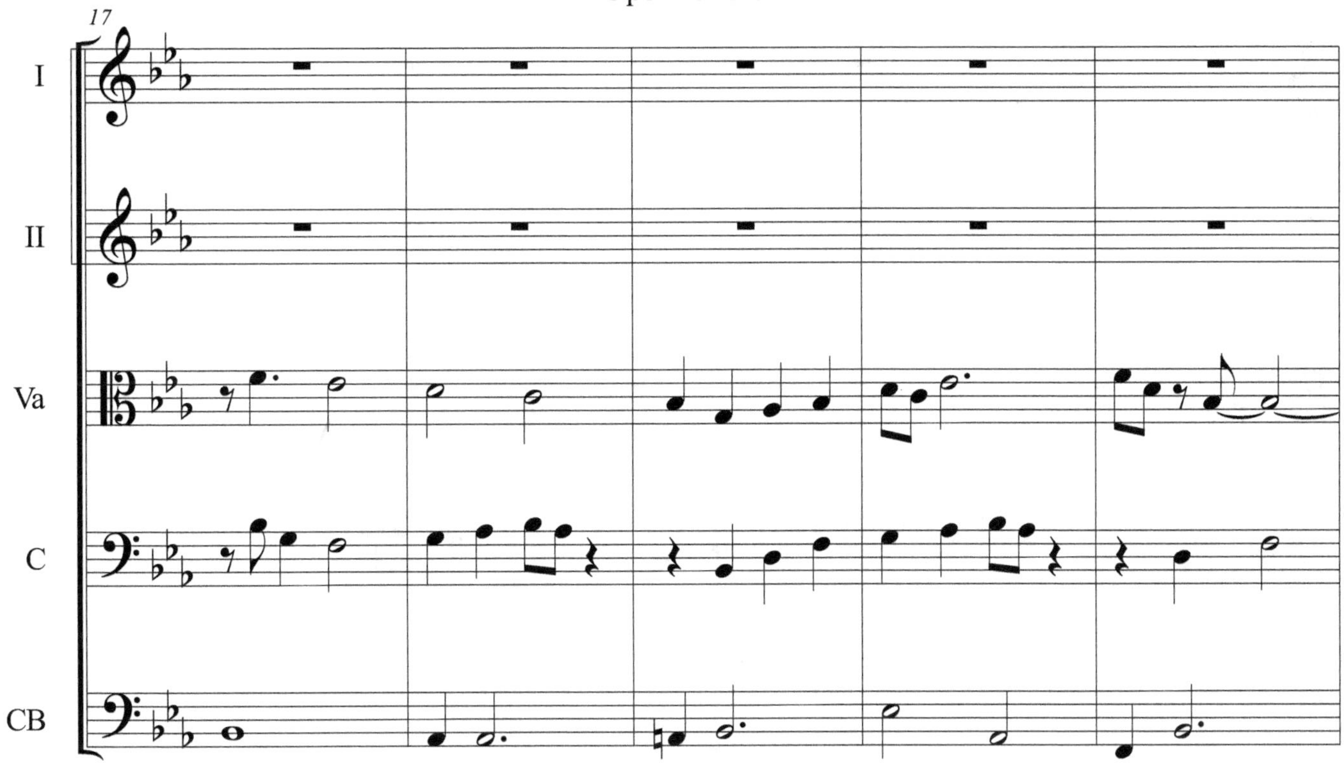
17
I
II
Va
C
CB

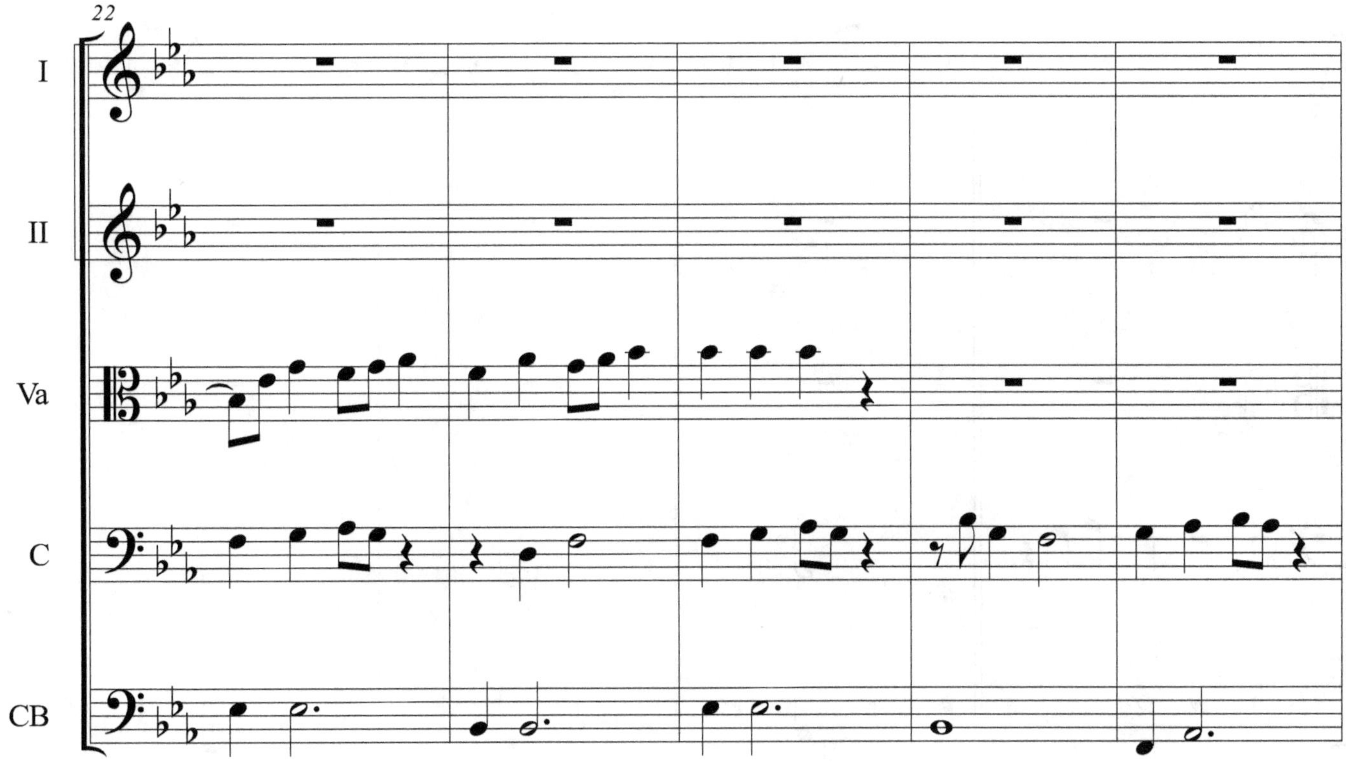
22
I
II
Va
C
CB

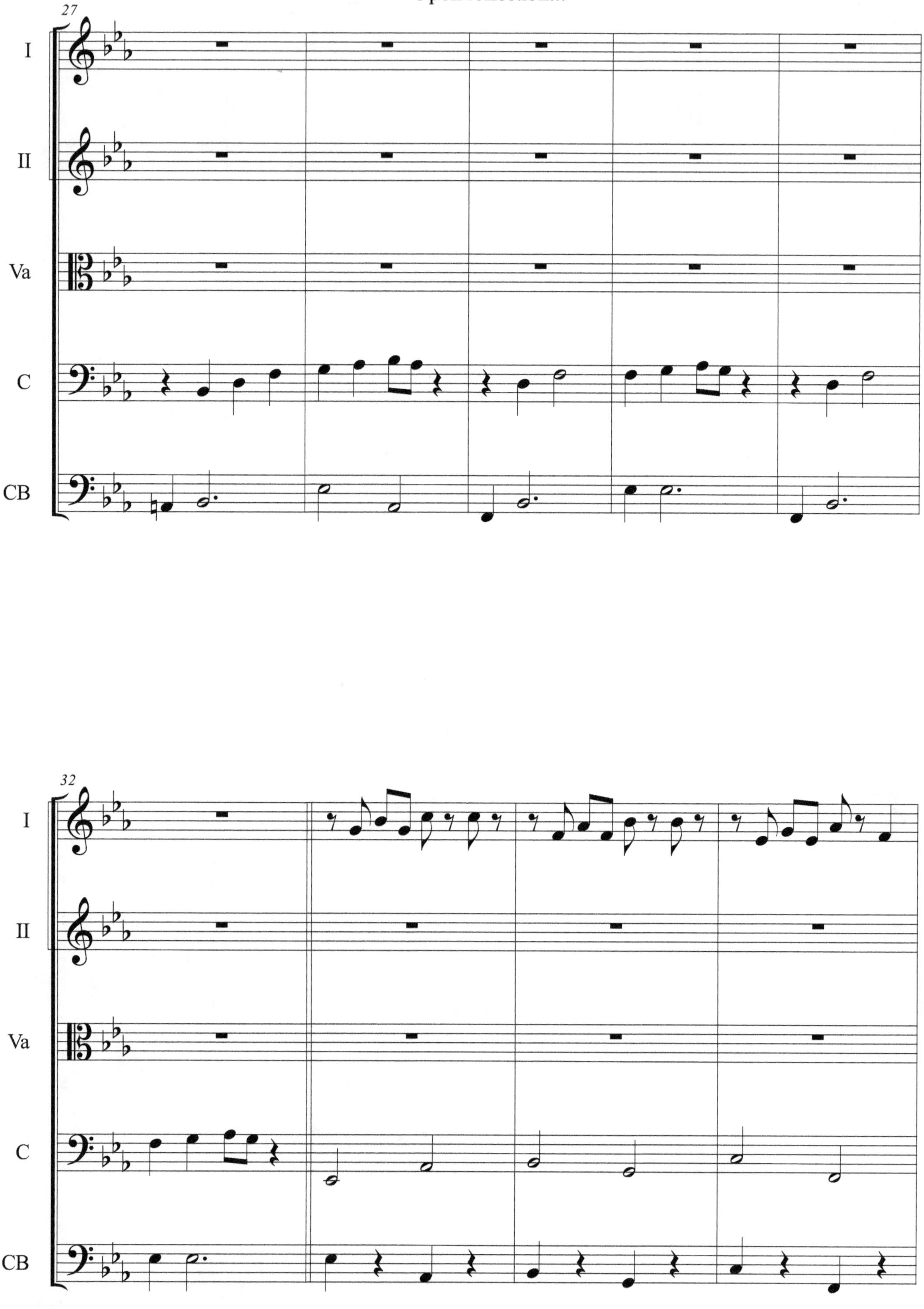
27
I
II
Va
C
CB
32
I
II
Va
C
CB

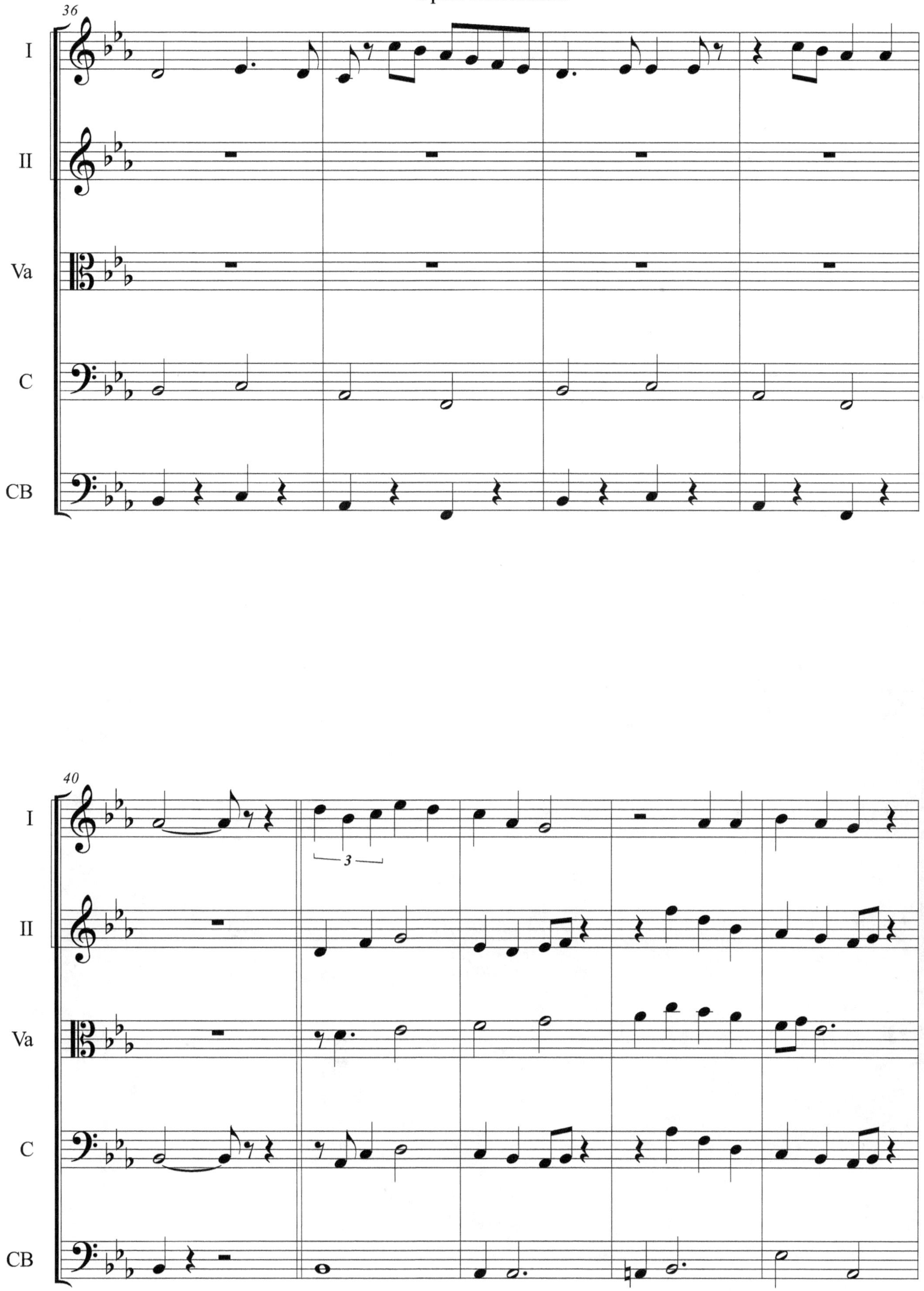
36
I
II
Va
C
CB
40
I
3
II
Va
C
CB

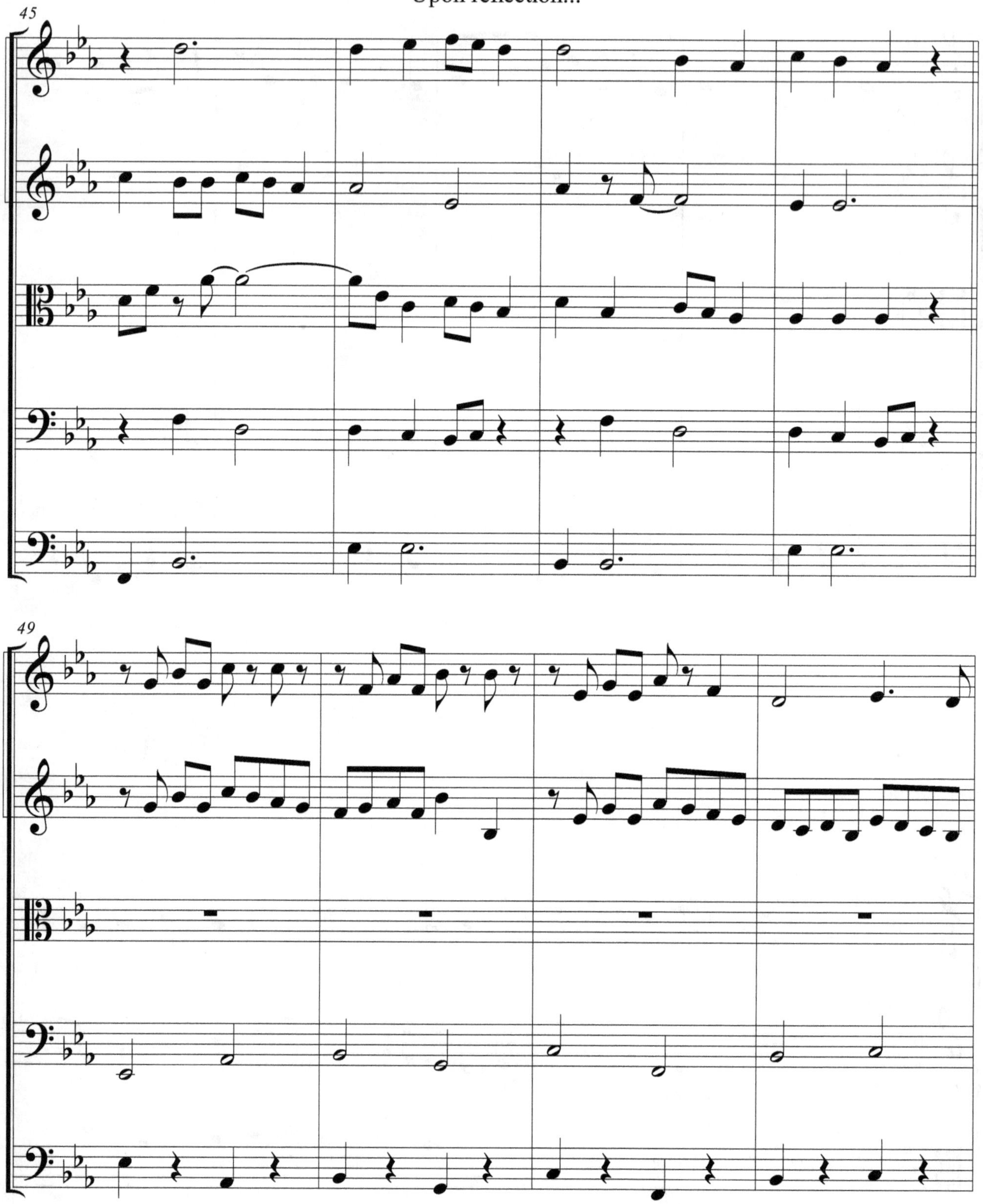
45
I
II
Va
C
CB
49
I
II
Va
C
CB

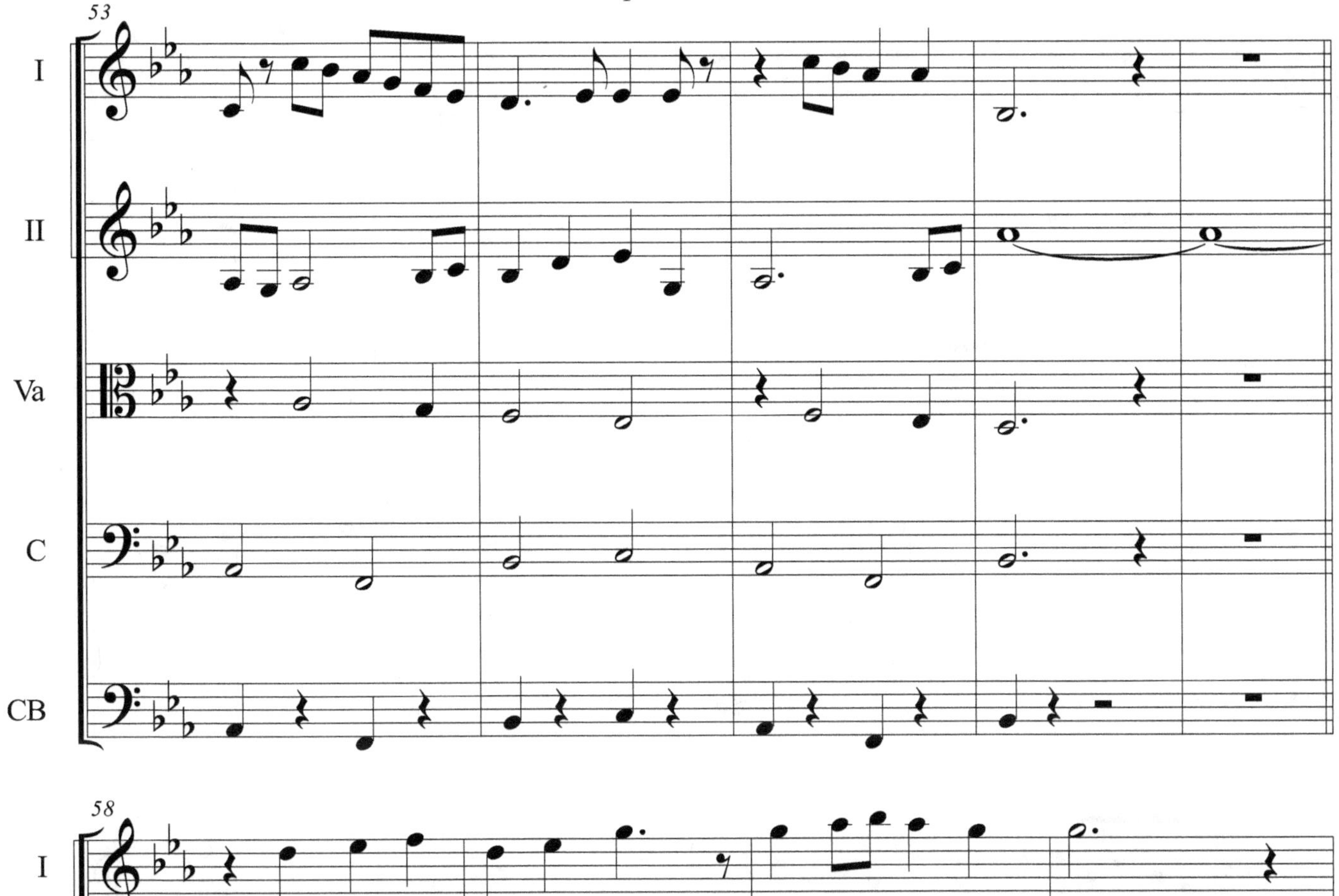
53
I
II
Va
C
CB
58
I
II
Va
C
CB

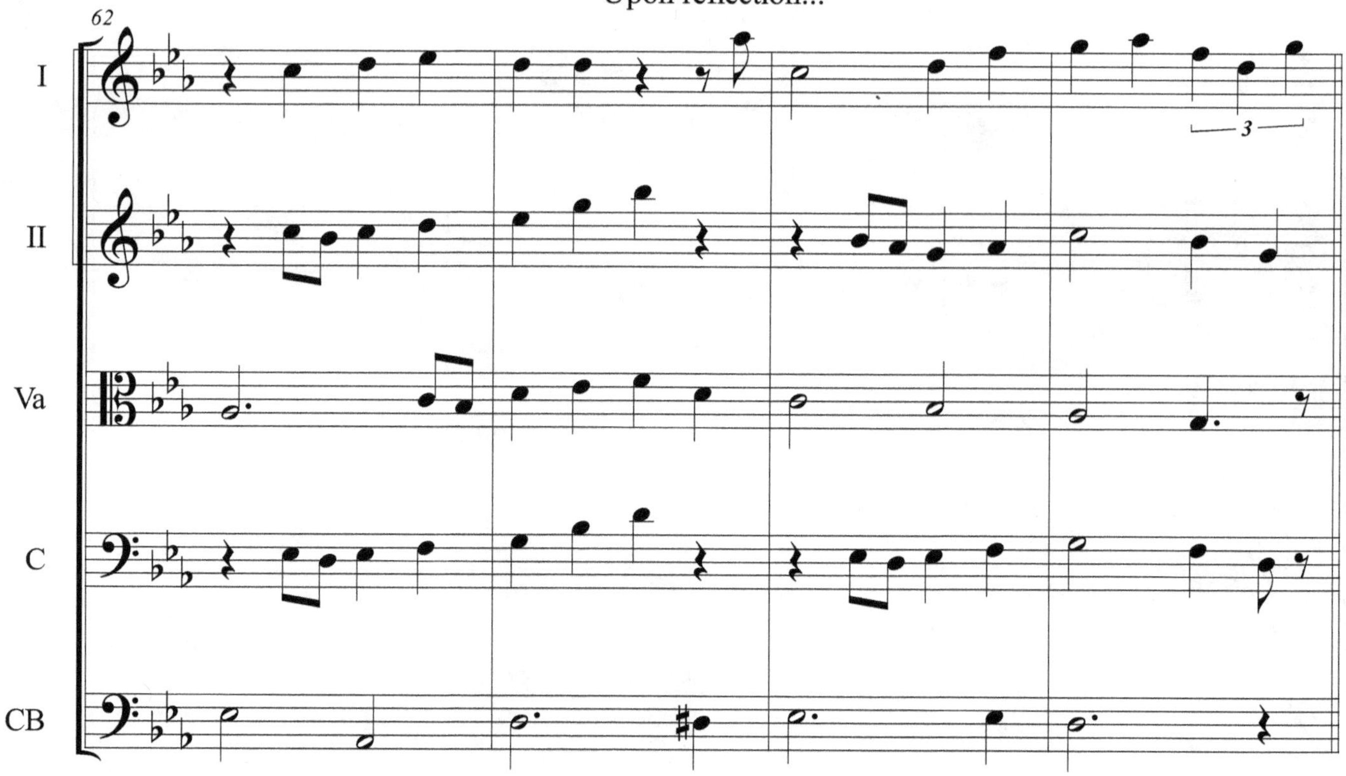
62
I
II
Va
C
CB
3

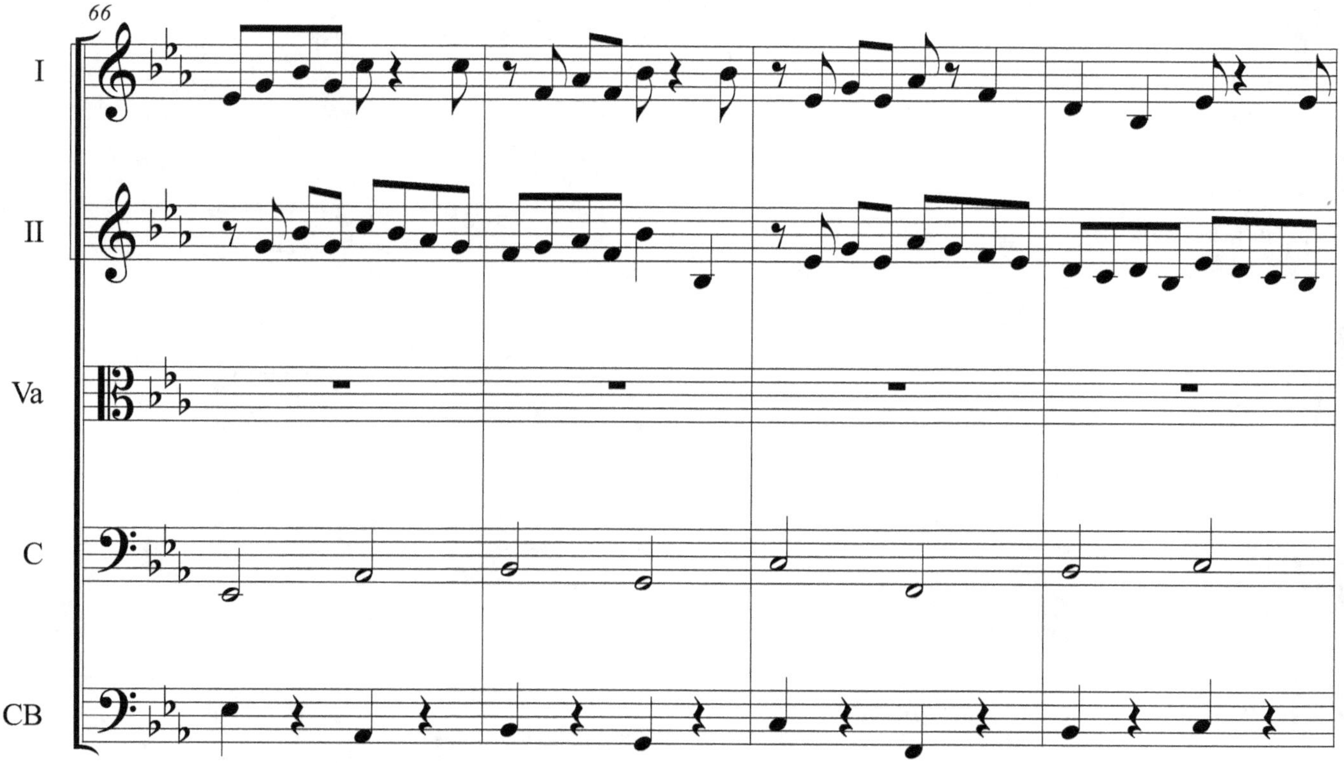
66
I
II
Va
C
CB

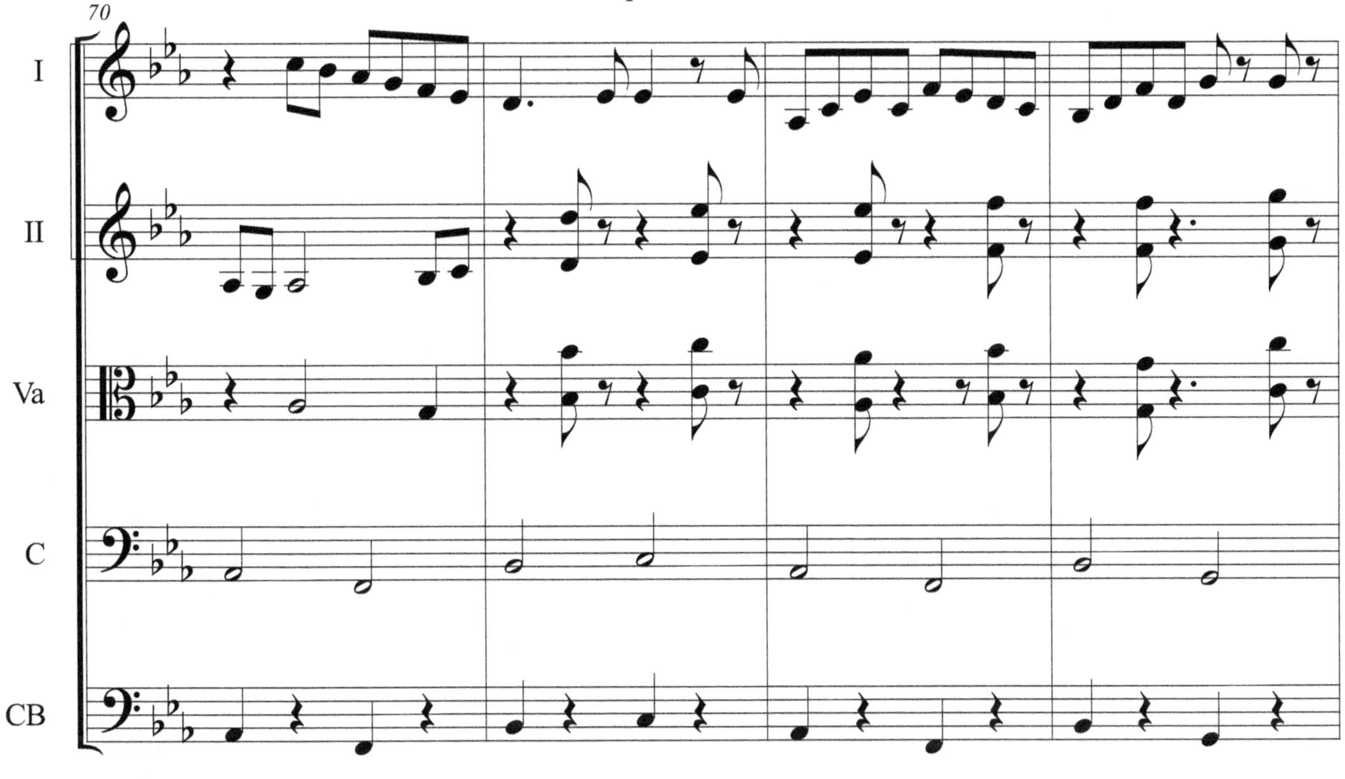
70
I
II
Va
C
CB

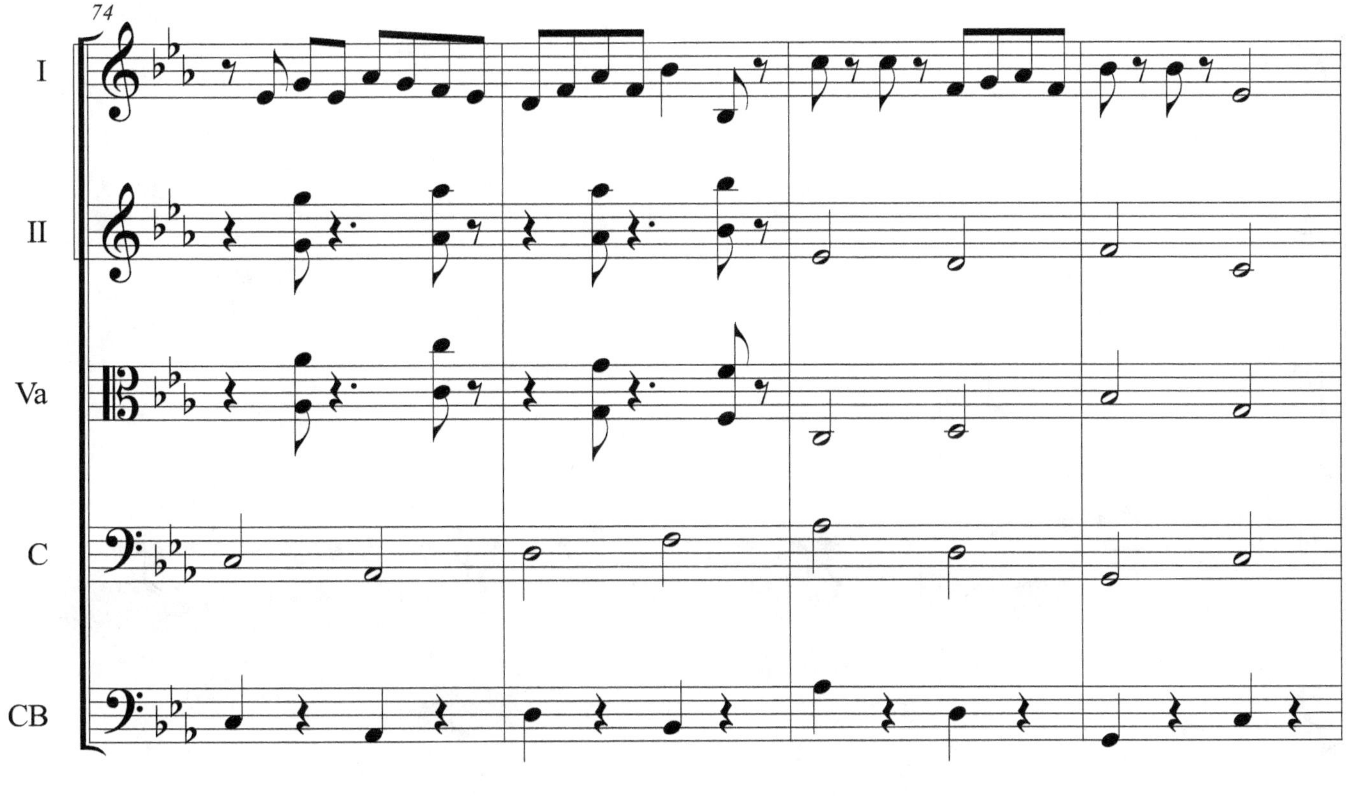
74
I
II
Va
C
CB

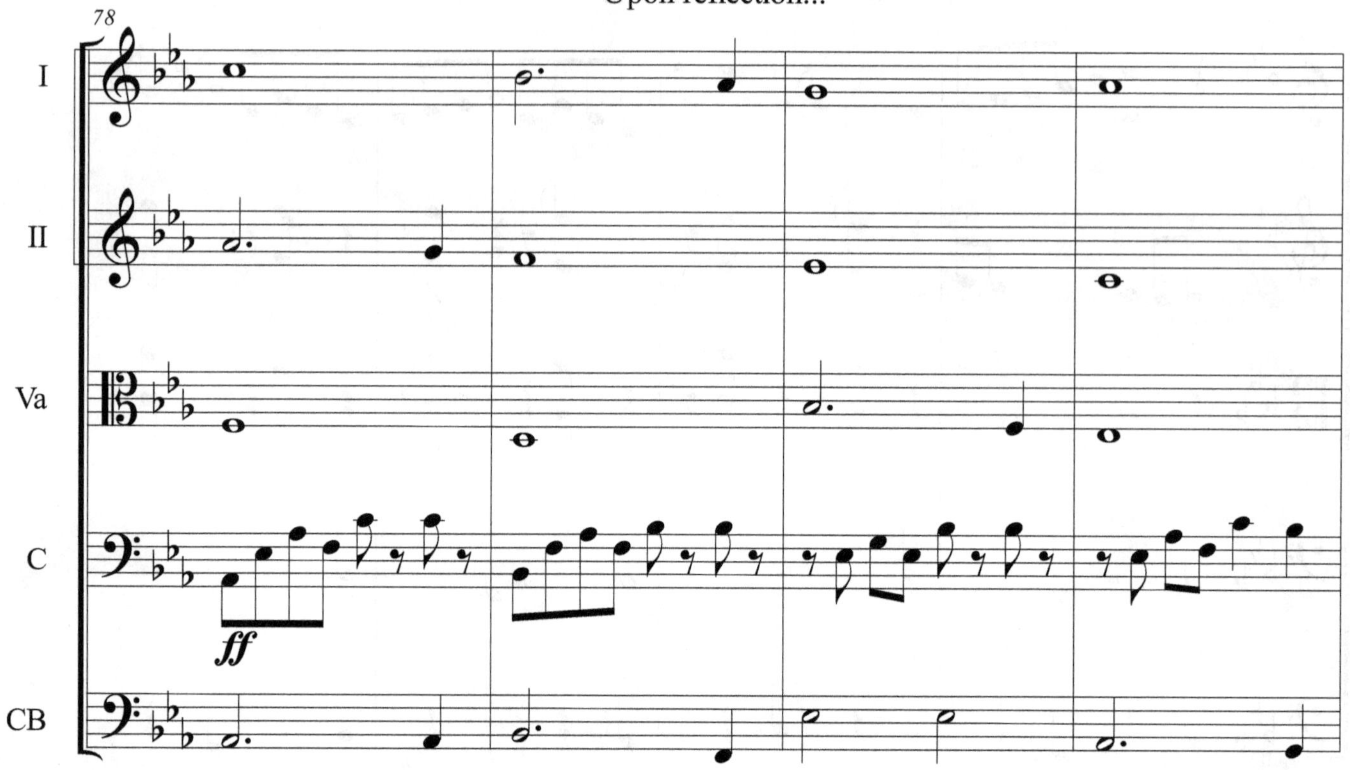
78
I
II
Va
C
ff
CB

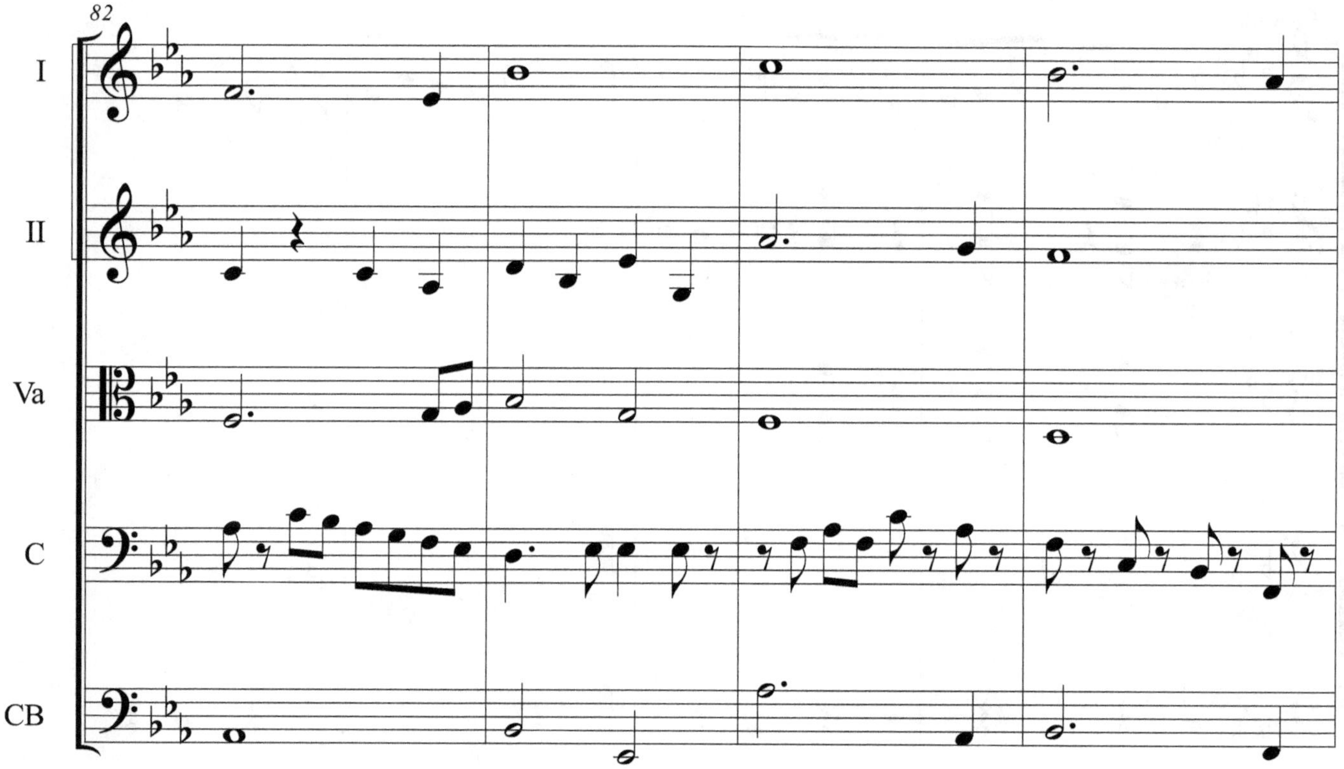
82
I
II
Va
C
CB

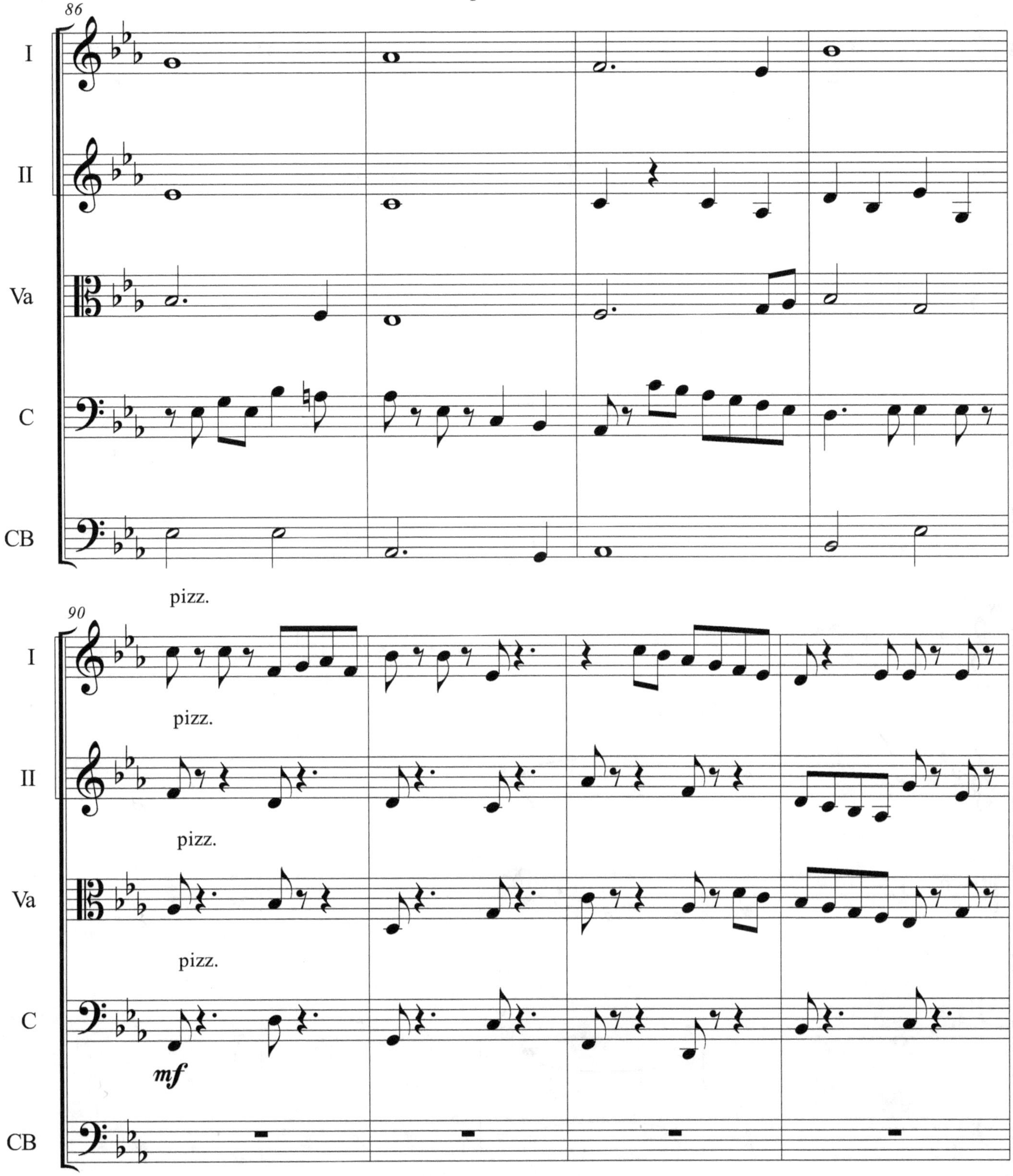
86
I
II
Va
C
CB
90
pizz.
pizz.
pizz.
pizz.
mf

Upon reflection...

68

Upon reflection...

69

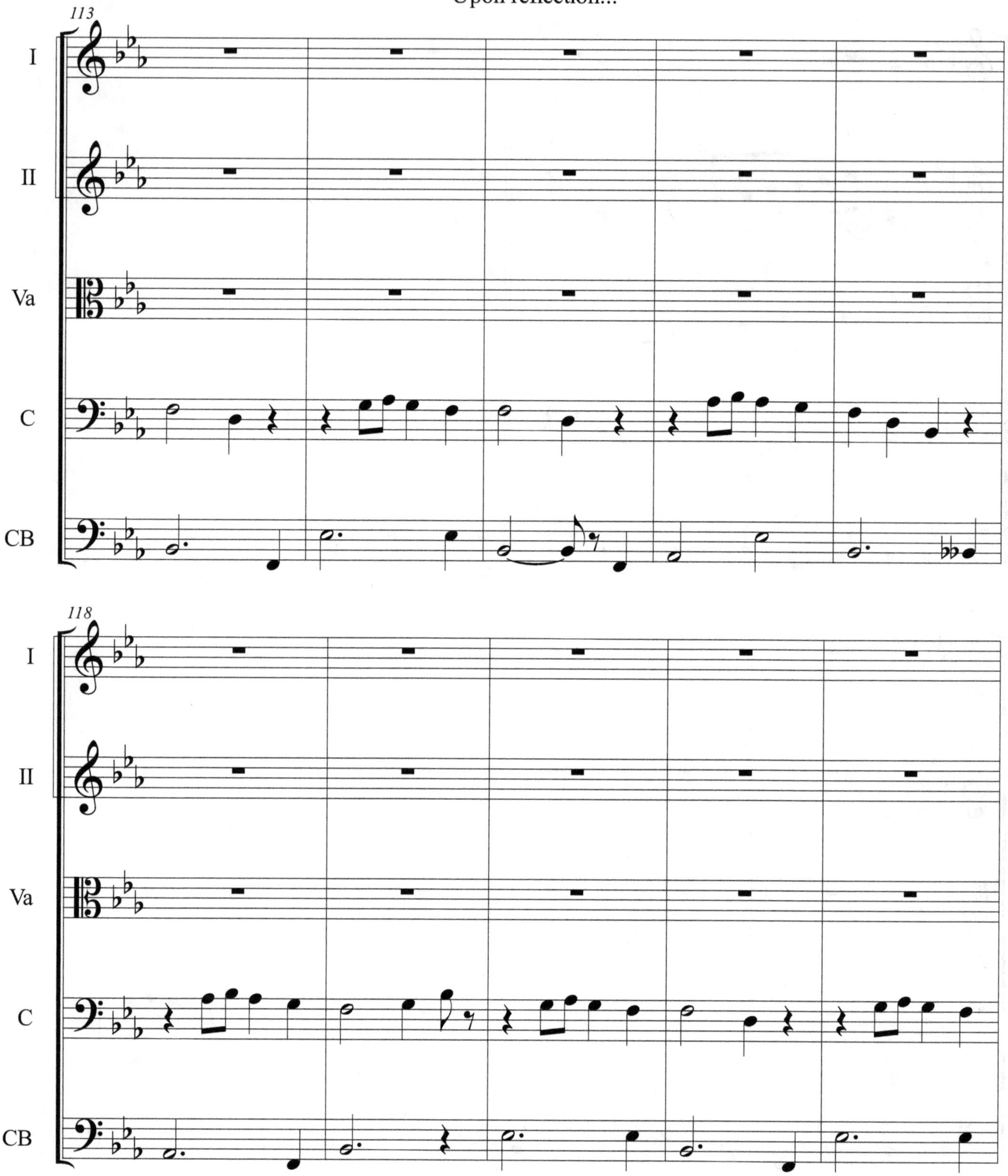
113
I
II
Va
C
CB
118
I
II
Va
C
CB

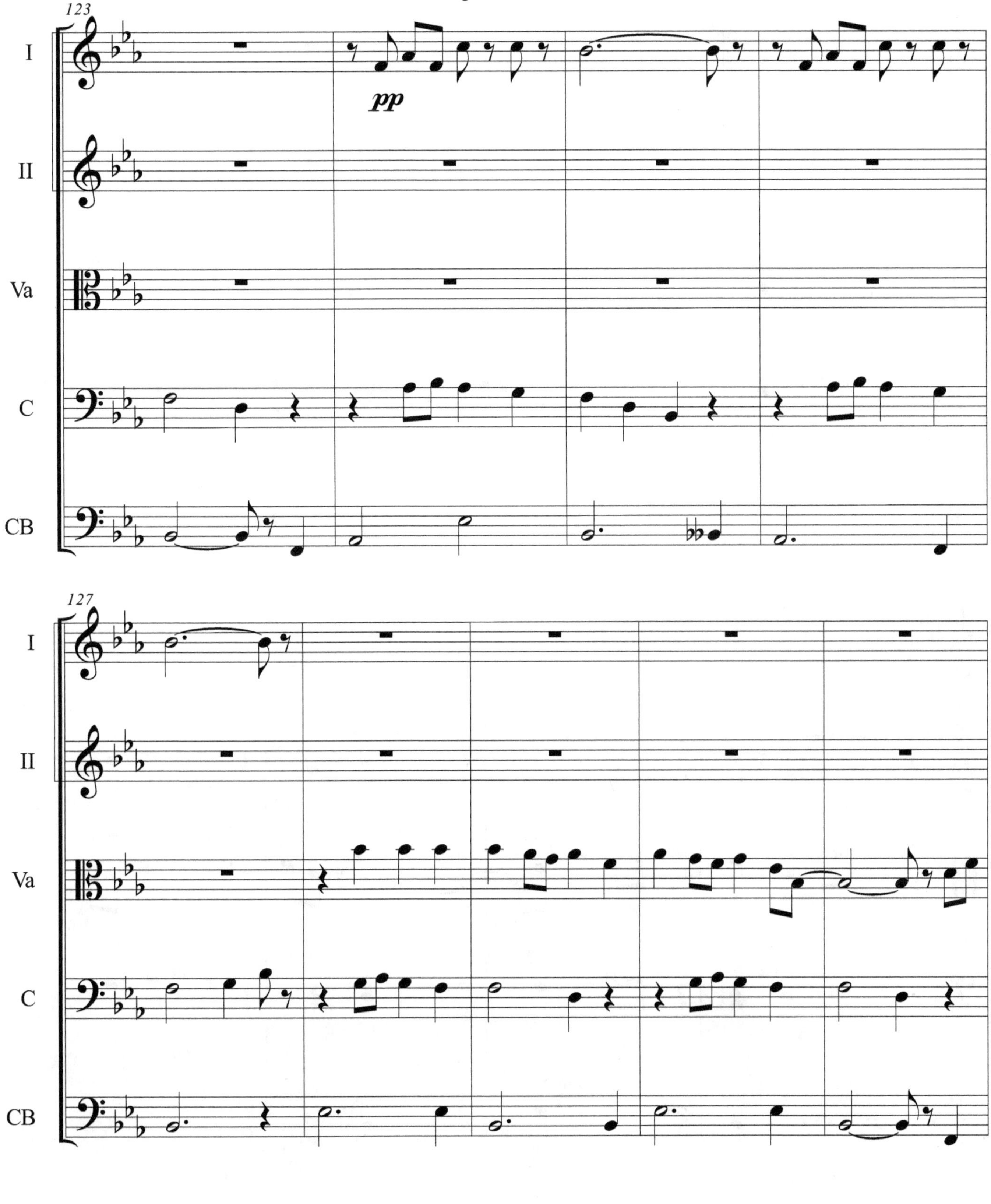
123
I
II
Va
C
CB
pp
127
I
II
Va
C
CB

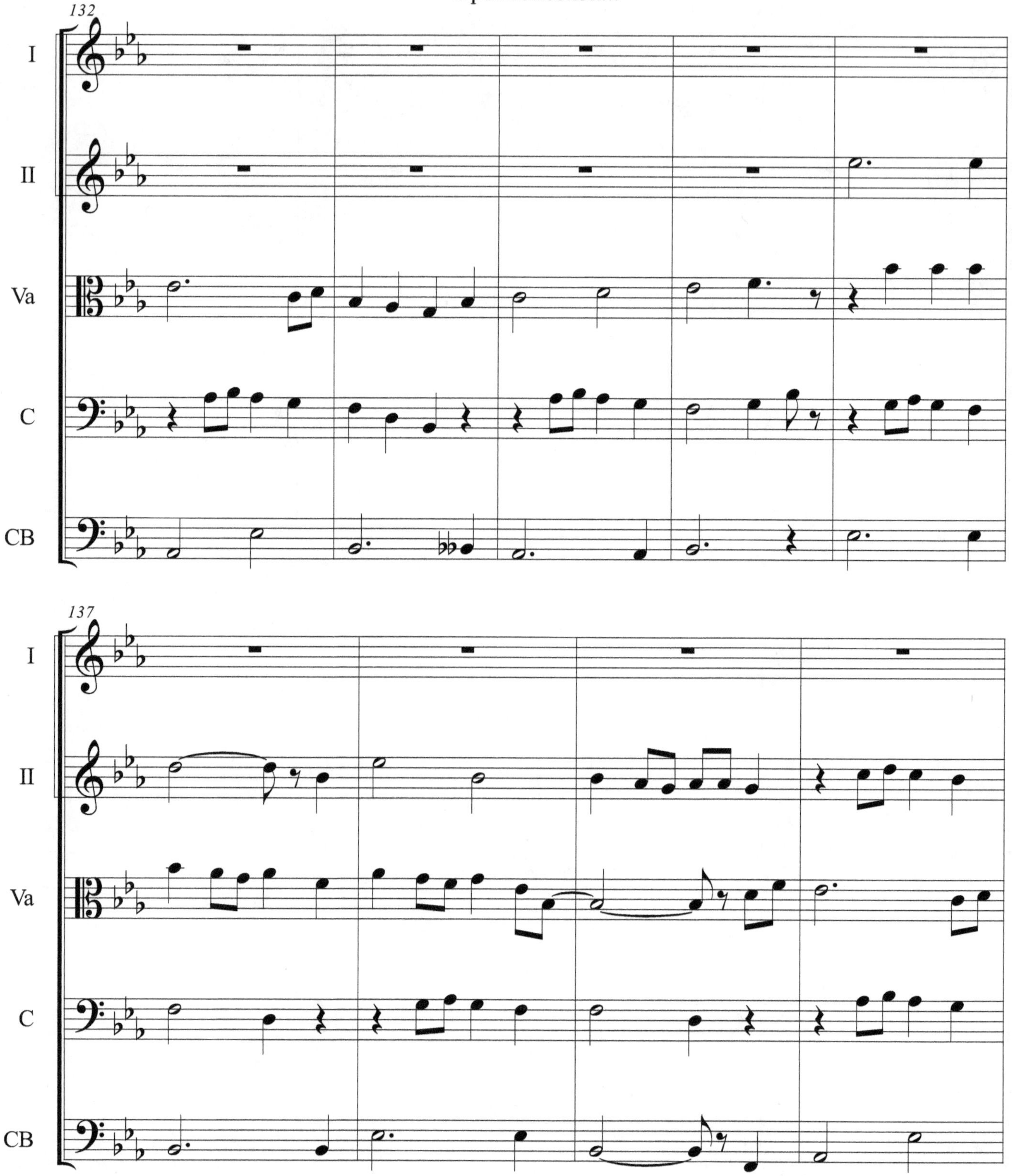
132
I
II
Va
C
CB
137
I
II
Va
C
CB

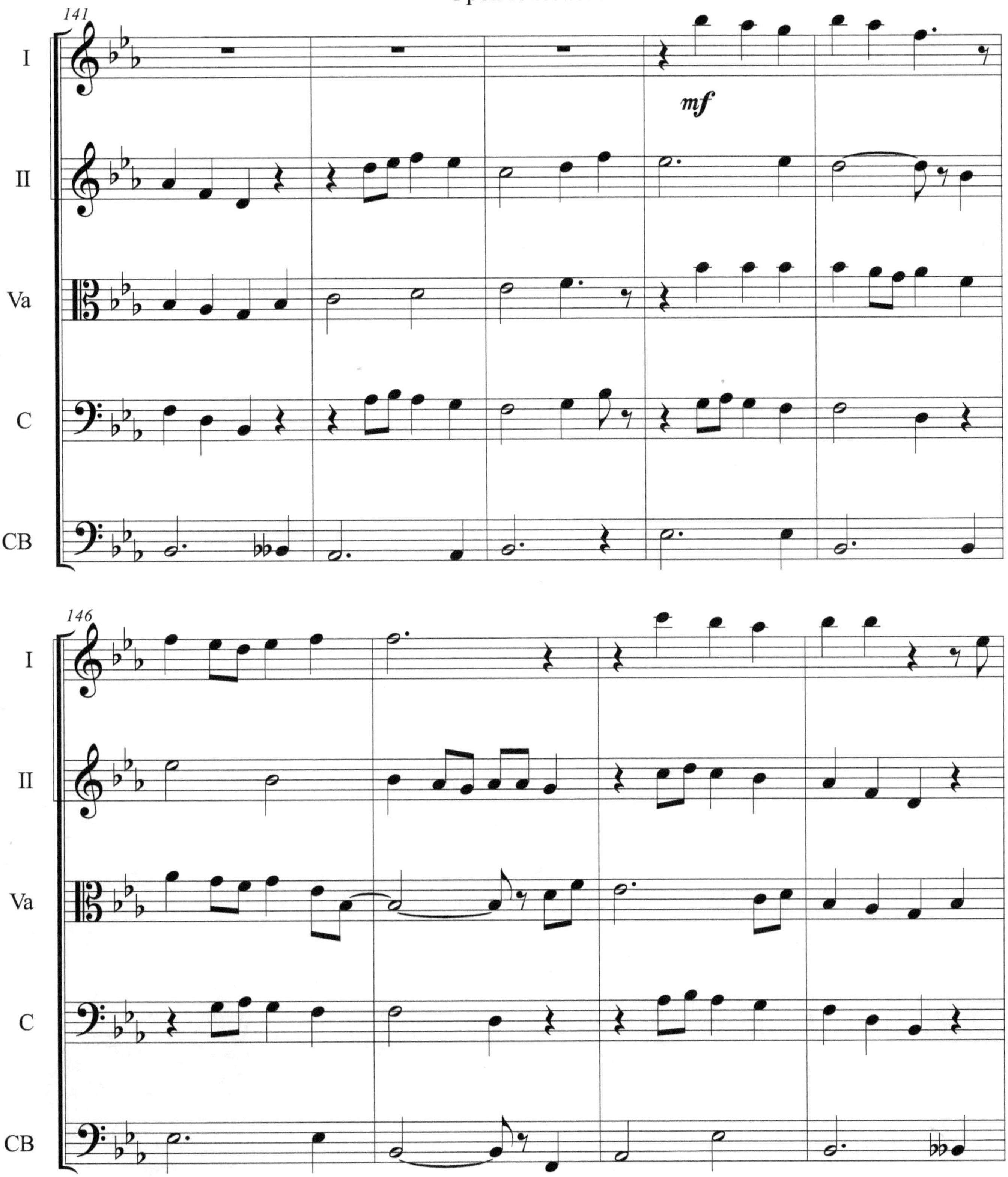
141
I
mf
II
Va
C
CB
146
I
II
Va
C
CB

Upon reflection...

Upon reflection...

HYPERCANON

*Quindici imagini della Madonna
con il viso di Maria Maddelena*

for string orchestra

•

by

Gerald Brennan
© 1987

Hypercanon

Quindici imagini della Madonna
con il viso di Maria Maddelena

Gerald Brennan

Play parts independently with great freedom and variety of tempo and dynamics;
③ at some point in each part, become tacet for a few seconds; movement ends when last player finishes.
Tutti con sordini, except basses.

56
4
Movement ends when last player finishes.
Moderato
Largo - pizzicato
Presto
Andante - tremolo
Allegro - portamento
Variable tempo
Andante
Allegro
Presto - pizzicato
Largo - tremolo
Variable tempo - portamento
Largo
Variable tempo - pizzicato
Allegro - tremolo
Andante - portamento
Vln. I 1
Vln. I 2
Vln. I 3
Vln. I 4
Vln. I 5
Vln. I 6
Vln. II 1
Vln. II 2
Vln. II 3
Vln. II 4
Vln. II 5
Vla. 1
Vla. 2
Vla. 3
Vla. 4
Vc. 1
Cb. 1

65
Vln. I 1
Vln. I 2
Vln. I 3
Vln. I 4
Vln. I 5
Vln. I 6
Vln. II 1
Vln. II 2
Vln. II 3
Vln. II 4
8va
Vln. II 5
Vla. 1
Vla. 2
Vla. 3
Vla. 4

Calmly; beautifully

5

83

Violins: Canon a 6; Senza misura; Con sordini; Entrances ad lib conductor's cue.
Cellos & Basses: moderato, in sync.
Movement ends when violin canon is finished.

146
8va
Vln. I 1
Vln. I 2
Vln. II 1
Vln. II 2
Cb. 1
157
9
Elegantly
Vln. I 1
Vln. I 2
Vln. II 1
Vln. II 2
Vc. 1
Cb. 1
168
Vc. 1
Cb. 1

180
10
pizz.
Vln. I 1
Vln. I 2
Vln. I 3
Vln. I 4
Vln. I 5
Vln. I 6
Vln. II 1
Vln. II 2
Vln. II 3
Vln. II 4
Vln. II 5
Vc. 1
Vc. 2
Vc. 3
Cb. 1

191
Vln. I 1
Vln. I 2
Vln. I 3
pizz.
Vln. I 4
pizz.
Vln. I 5
Vln. I 6
Vln. II 1
tr
8va
3
Vln. II 2
pizz.
tr
8va
Vln. II 3
tr
pizz.
8va
Vln. II 4
tr
pizz.
Vln. II 5
tr
8va
Vc. 1
Vc. 2
pizz.
Vc. 3
Cb. 1

199
Vln. I 1
Vln. I 2
Vln. I 3
Vln. I 4
Vln. I 5
Vln. I 6
Vln. II 1
Vln. II 2
Vln. II 3
Vln. II 4
Vln. II 5
Vc. 1
Vc. 2
Vc. 3
Cb. 1
8va
random pizz.
pizz.
arco

210
Vln. I 1
Vln. I 2
Vln. I 3
Vln. I 4
Vln. I 5
Vln. I 6
Vln. II 1
Vln. II 2
Vln. II 3
Vln. II 4
Vln. II 5
Vc. 1
Vc. 2
Vc. 3
Cb. 1
arco

218
(8va)
Vln. I 1
Vln. I 2
Vln. I 3
Vln. I 4
Vln. I 5
Vln. I 6
Vln. II 1
Vln. II 2
Vln. II 3
Vln. II 4
Vln. II 5
Vla. 1
Vc. 1
Vc. 2
Vc. 3
Cb. 1
arco
arco
arco
arco
arco
11
227
Vln. I 1
Vla. 1
Cb. 1

239
Vln. I 1
Vla. 1
Cb. 1
253
12
Vln. I 1
Vln. I 2
Vln. I 3
Vln. I 4
Vln. I 5
Vln. I 6
Vla. 1
Vc. 1
Vc. 2
Vc. 3
Cb. 1

265
Vln. I 1
Vln. I 2
Vln. I 3
Vln. I 4
Vln. I 5
Vln. I 6
Vc. 1
Vc. 2
Vc. 3
Cb. 1
8va
13
Vla. 1
Cb. 1
289
14
Vla. 1
Vla. 2
Vla. 3
Vla. 4
Vc. 1
Vc. 2
Vc. 3
Cb. 1
tr

300
Vla. 1
Vla. 2
Vla. 3
Vla. 4
Vc. 1
Vc. 2
Vc. 3
Cb. 1
308
cadenza first violinist
Vln. I 1
Vla. 1
Vla. 2
Vla. 3
Vla. 4
Vc. 1
Vc. 2
Vc. 3
Cb. 1
15
Prelude
Vln. I 1
Vla. 1
Vc. 1
Cb. 1

16 **Finale**

327
8va tremolo
Vln. I 1
Vln. I 2
Vln. I 3
Vln. I 4
Vln. I 5
Vln. I 6
Vln. II 1
Vln. II 2
Vln. II 3
Vln. II 4
Vln. II 5
Vla. 1
Vla. 2
Vla. 3
Vla. 4
Vc. 1
Vc. 2
Vc. 3
Cb. 1
Cb. 2
Con sord.
f
p
mf

338
8va
Vln. I 1
Vln. I 2
Vln. I 3
Vln. I 4
Vln. I 5
Vln. I 6
Vln. II 1
Vln. II 2
Vln. II 3
Vln. II 4
Vln. II 5
Vla. 1
Vla. 2
Vla. 3
Vla. 4
Vc. 1
Vc. 2
Vc. 3
Cb. 1
Cb. 2

ANTICANON

•

by
Gerald Brennan
© 2022

to

Sam Morgen

a woman with Asperger's Syndrome whom I invented in a novel
to show me how to write the Anticanon

The study of form
is the result of man's inability to sustain ecstasy.

&

Never tell someone *how* to do something.
Tell them *what* to do
and you will be astonished by their ingenuity.
– US General George Patton

&

Poets to come! orators, singers, musicians to come!
Not to-day is to justify me and answer what I am for,
But you, a new brood, native, athletic, continental, greater than
before known, Arouse! for you must justify me.
I myself but write one or two indicative words for the future,
I but advance a moment only to wheel
and hurry back in the darkness.
I am a man who, sauntering along without fully stopping,
Turns a casual look upon you and then averts his face,
Leaving it to you to prove and define it,
Expecting the main things from you.
– Walt Whitman

THE EVOLUTION OF THE ANTICANON

The essence of the *Anticanon*, as it was first given to me, and indeed, has persisted, is that each instrument of the orchestra shall be independent in note content, meter, tempo, and key. I originally envisioned a band of 100 players – a typical large modern orchestra. Each player's part was to be without few rests, that is, each player was engaged throughout the 30-minute piece.

Overall unity of the *Anticanon* is provided by the *synchronistic illumination of content*; in other words, everyone is playing something different, but everyone is telling the same story from their unique point of view. I employed this chart I call the Emotion Wheel:

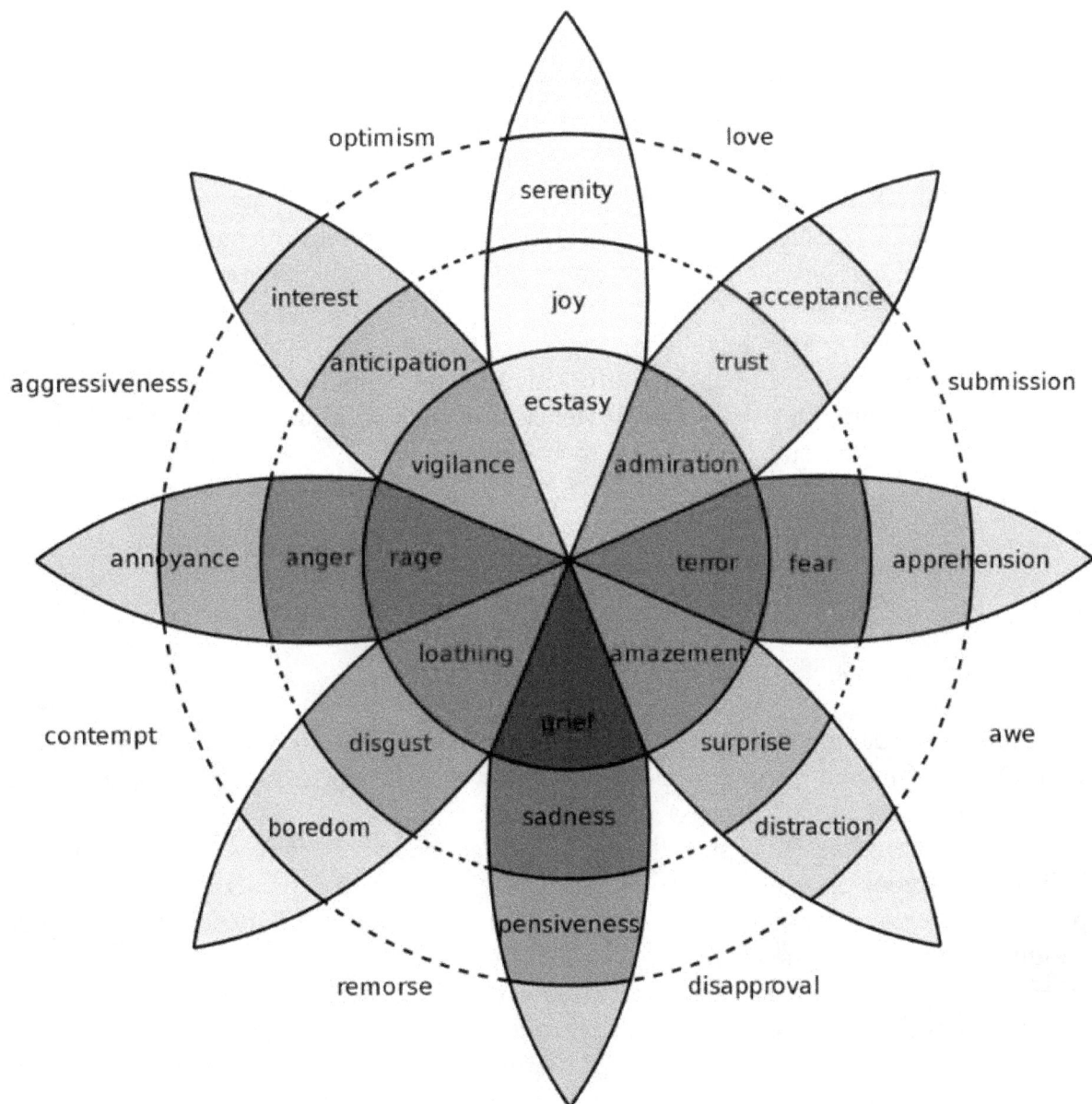

From this chart, I chose a progression of emotional states. But it was only one of a combination of zillions of possible combinations. (The numbers indicate duration of each section.):

:

1. Apprehension (2)
2. Fear (4)
3. Growing Anger (2)
4. Shock (1)
5. Desolation (2)
6. Grief and Misery (4)
7. Loving Memories (4)
8. Acceptance (2)
9. Joy (6)
10. Finale: Ecstasy (2)

Two problems, intractable, soon raised their ugly heads.

- Did I really want the brass and percussion playing without rest throughout the piece? Any way my mind played it, it was raucous and ugly. Yet the idea of everyone playing throughout was, and is, part of the very essence of the work.
- Did I really want to write 100 30-minute pieces of music? That's a lifetime body of work that would likely take the ginger out of me for the rest of my time on planet Earth. So, no. I didn't.

It became obvious, eventually, that the only sounds I could stand listening to for a full half-hour would be from the strings. And I needed, for my own sanity, to scale the piece down to a workload I found realistic. So, the piece became:

for strings
20 violins
12 violas
8 cellos
4 basses

And, as I needed the work to remain a substantial edifice, I kept the 30-minute idea. This sorts well with the duration of other important string works as we have from Dvorak, Tchaikovsky, R. Strauss, etc.

Another original essential spec for the piece was the idea of *spotlighting*. Unless your score indicates that your part is being spotlit, one always plays in dynamics ranging from *p* to *mp*. Spotlit parts come to the fore, at the discretion of the player. Anywhere between 0 and 44 parts may be spotlit at times during the piece.

How is spotlighting administered? This is key. Each performance has a different pattern of who gets spotlit and for what duration. This way the piece can be heard multiple times, keep the same progression of emotional states (as in the example above) yet never sound the same from one performance to another. One may opt for a computer generated grid indicating the spotlight template for a particular performance, or it may be drawn up manually by the conductor or a designate. In the revised version, which we shall discuss below, it is also allowable that this spotlighting process is done *ad lib* and in real time by the players.

With all this in mind, I had tried dozens of times in the past ten years to put pen to paper and do this thing. Something always stopped me. I loved the general idea but there was something essentially out-of-whack about how I was going about implementing the essential kernel, the inner essence of the *Anticanon* concept. I was stumped.

* * * * *

I am a novelist. In my novel *The Angel Jophiel,* a composer named Bran Englander (which is an anagram of my name) writes the *Anticanon,* but for full orchestra. (He must be an awesome composer because I could never make that happen to my satisfaction.) In a subsequent novel, *Sam Morgen* (which I am in the process of finishing, God willing), Bran's Asperger's Syndrome daughter, Samantha Morgen Englander (Sam Morgen), tells her world famous father that his version is imperfect. She insists that she knows how to fully unlock the potential of Bran's idea. This causes a great rift in their relationship. Sam is socially very inept; indeed, Bran, even after decades of submitting to the discipline of tolerating his daughter's searing honesty, can't help but be hurt by her insinuation that his work is defective.

And when I realized what Sam had done, her perfection of her father's work, and deemed it to be true, I knew that I had to change my own approach to create the actual *Anticanon.*

What did Sam do? She kept the map of emotional states but realized that the scheme that her father had implemented was just one of about $2.6313083693369E+35$ possible schemes. But to acknowledge the existence of all these possible combinations also meant that it became impossible to write music for all the emotional states on the chart due to the many choices of timings allowed for each section. Plus, transitions and segues between states would have to be ignored—each state could segue into as many as 31 others.

Sam also kept the core concepts of independence in note content, meter, tempo, and key. She agreed that the 30-minute duration was a good length for a large string orchestra, but what if a wind quintet wanted to implement the core features of the *Anticanon* concept for a 10-minute performance? Could not the same rules be applied to a smaller ensemble, even a soloist?

And, if you haven't already guessed, Sam's big departure from Bran's original idea was to only write for *musicians,* not mere score-readers. She made the analogy that novelists are different from typists, just as musicians are different from score-readers. Most 'classical' musicians? Take away their scores and they are mute.

So, Sam took away the idea that real musicians require a printed score made by someone else in order to represent a progression of emotional states. Once the group of musicians (however the group is constituted) agree on a scheme of emotional progression taken from the master Emotion Wheel, and decide the length of each emotional episode, they are ready to play the piece. The *spotlighting* idea is no longer required, as the piece is played by actual musicians who know how to listen to one another, give generously and take heartily at the right moments. And still—each performance of the 'same' work, even with the same musicians and emotional progression, will sound completely different from another performance.

Yes, when we talk here about real musicians, we are talking about the ability to *improvise* within an ensemble of other real musicians. It's not as unreasonable a requirement as it might seem—Jazz has been doing this for a century, why not orchestras? It is time, Sam contended, that we pay more attention to the musicians than to the score-readers.

Bran countered that his piece was *not* defective because it was written to include the vast majority of orchestral musicians in orchestras throughout the world. Inclusiveness to Bran was a virtue. Not so to his daughter. Sam, an elitist to her bones, argued that the true essence of Bran's idea leads to a freedom of expression within a concise framework that was revolutionary in its structure and flexibility. To Sam, Bran's original concept, though innovative enough to send an earthquake through the classical music world, was but a half-measure. Bran maintained that very few orchestra musicians were able to improvise within a larger ensemble; Sam agreed but countered that this condition was an unavoidable consequence of the perfected idea.

I learned a lot from Sam. The score of the *Anticanon* follows.

CR

THE ANTICANON
Score Notes

1. Overall unity of the *Anticanon* is provided by the *synchronistic illumination of content;* in other words, everyone is playing something different, but *everyone is telling the same story* from their unique point of view.

2. A progression of emotional states is selected from the Emotion Wheel illustrated below. That is the source for the preparation of the template for all the participants to be bound to in that particular performance.

3. Length of each section, each illustrated emotional state, must be predetermined. Players must keep track of each sections duration and execute a viable transition to the next section. Any number of emotional sections may be included in a particular performance. But be thoughtful about the number of sections explored and the time allotted to each.

4. The *Anticanon* may be arranged for any number of players, from solo to full orchestra.

5. What music is made is the responsibility of the players. It must not be written out. Each player illuminates the designated emotional state under consideration while listening to the rest of the group. This experience cannot be predicted and therefore must be a product of the moment.

6. Meter, tempo and key is always an individual decision. The only synchronization to consider is the synchronization of the emotional content as indicated by the title of the section being played, and the synchronization of the timings allotted to the expression of each emotional state in the progression. I oughtn't still be playing a part, the timing of which has expired, while the others have paid better attention and have moved on to next section.

7. This is not easy to play well. One must get one's own point-of-view across while listening to all the others. This is a unique approach to ensemble playing. In the classical orchestra world, improvisation was permitted only in the cadenzas of concertos. Here each player may indulge him or herself to an unprecedented degree, but one needs to temper this impulse by listening to what is happening with the rest of the ensemble at all times. Simple universal rule for ensemble improvisation: Don't be a wallflower, but don't hog the spotlight.

8. A note about dynamics. Most of the time, unless one is urged on from within, it is best to stay in the background and let another, or others, come to the fore when they feel the need to do so. The *Anticanon* calls for great restraint, and also great courage to come forth when moved by the spirit.

9. The *Anticanon* is elite music. There are few musicians these days who are up to the task. As humanity evolves their tribe shall increase, and a new chapter in the evolution of human arts may be written.

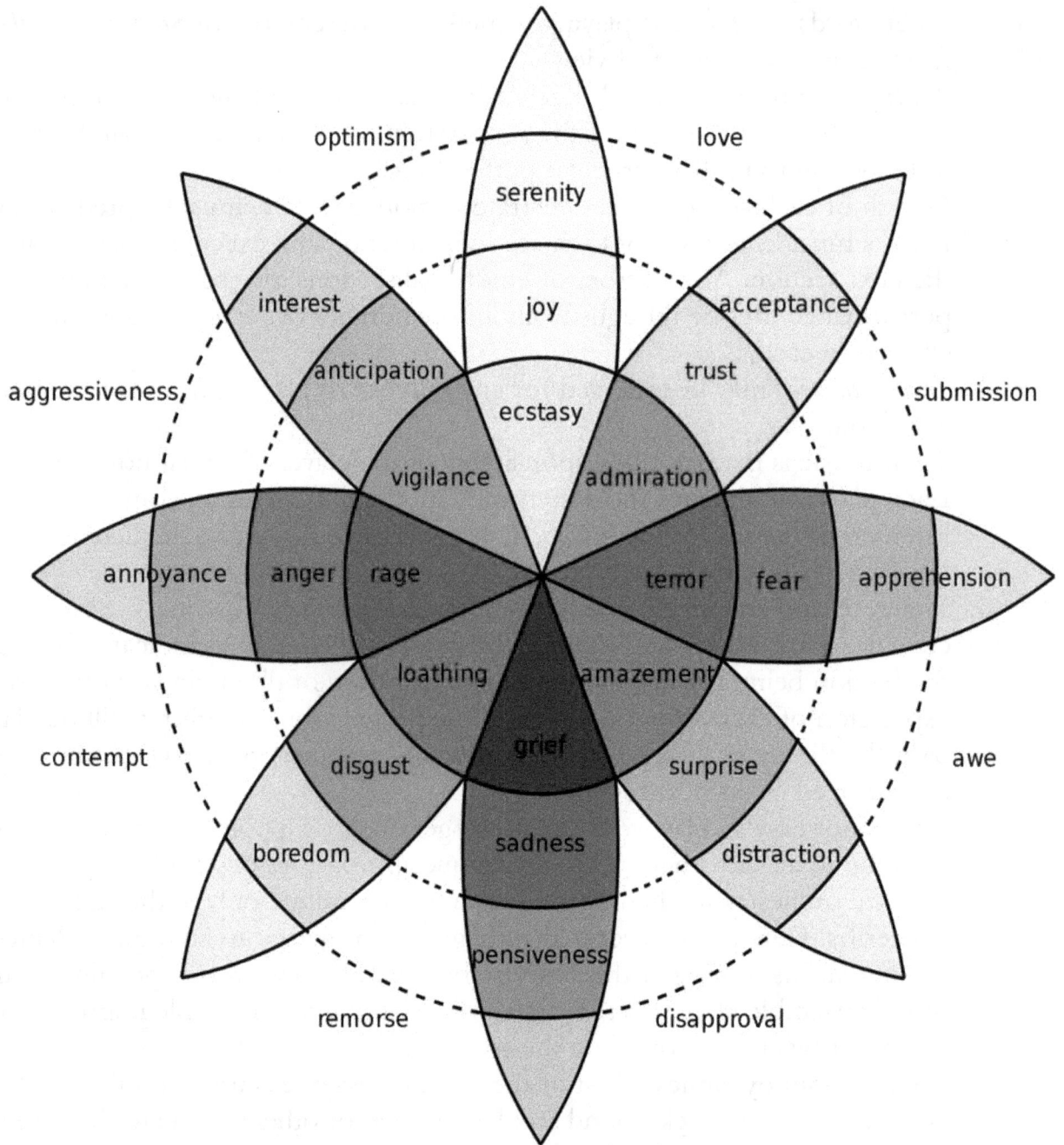

THE ANTICANON
Sample Scores

Sample#1

for strings
20 violins
12 violas
8 cellos
4 basses

30 minutes

In ten sections:
1) Apprehension (2)
2) Fear (4)
3) Growing Anger (2)
4) Shock (1)
5) Desolation (2)
6) Grief and Misery (4)
7) Loving Memories (4)
8) Acceptance (2)
9) Joy (6)
10) Finale: Ecstasy (2)

Sample#2

for wind quintet
2 flutes
Oboe
Clarinet
Bassoon

10 minutes

In five sections:
1) Boredom (2)
2) Anger (1)
3) Surprise (1)
4) Admiration (2)
5) Serenity (4)